"David Jeffrey's latest book . . . is a mingled yarn about the extraordinary-ordinary people who set him straight on life's path. Rural and urban, Christian and pagan, lettered or life-wise, every one of the 'real characters' we meet in these pages left their trace on this masterful storyteller's wide and tender understanding."

—GRAEME HUNTER
University of Ottawa

"*Real Characters* is not just great storytelling; it is a refreshing introduction to genuine folk who don't find it necessary to live up to other people's expectations. . . . Among the characters . . . there is one whose own life threads through them all—David Jeffrey, who in these reminiscences reveals his own quirks and passions for learning, love, and faith."

—PAUL W. GOOCH
Victoria University in the University of Toronto

"Whether in the Ottawa Valley of his youth, the ivory towers of Princeton, or a Florentine *trattoria*, David Jeffrey shows that the Front Porch Republic isn't just limited to American small towns or rural homesteads. Porchers everywhere will want to 'sit a spell' with Jeffrey for his delightful and moving stories of the 'real characters' who made him the man he is."

—SCOTT H. MOORE
Baylor University

"This is a delightful and most pleasurable book. It brought back memories of some nonconforming individuals that I have known over the past sixty-plus years. I wholeheartedly and enthusiastically endorse *Real Characters*."

—BILL ROBBINS
Business leader and major financial supporter
of Christian colleges and universities

"David Jeffrey is a lad from the Ottawa Valley, a curious lost Canadian landscape where, over the centuries, the law of gravity seems to have been inconsistently understood and applied. The resultant misfits who have graced the place are some of the subjects brought to light in this book. These oddballs from the ozone populate the pages of this scholarly and tractor-friendly tome."

—RAY CORRIN
Health Canada

REAL CHARACTERS

REAL CHARACTERS

A Tip of the Hat to Nonconformity

David Lyle Jeffrey

Front Porch Republic *Books*

REAL CHARACTERS
A Tip of the Hat to Nonconformity

Front Porch Republic
An Imprint of Wipf and Stock Publishers
199 W. 8th Ave., Suite 3
Eugene, OR 97401

www.wipfandstock.com

PAPERBACK ISBN: 978-1-7252-8109-7
HARDCOVER ISBN: 978-1-7252-8108-0
EBOOK ISBN: 978-1-7252-8110-3

Manufactured in the U.S.A.   SEPTEMBER 28, 2020

For Joshua, who even more than his mother, insisted that I finally get to work and write some of these stories down.

CONTENTS

ACKNOWLEDGEMENTS

I SHOULD LIKE TO thank the editors of *Touchstone* for allowing me to revise "One Good Teacher" from their September 2017 issue; it appears here as "Pop Shaver." Also appearing here as "Sadie and Lawson" is a trio of poems first published by *Local Culture* in the spring issue for 2020. All other material appears here for the first time in print, though doubtless my children, students, and forbearing friends will protest they have heard much of it before, and more than once.

INTRODUCTION

It will be apparent to anyone interested in reading this little book that our contemporary world is peopled with folk who can seem pretty homogenous, apparently mass-produced. Unsurprisingly, it is the rarer, eccentric personalities that typically we remember longest, not only because they stand out, but because they more often make us think a new thought. I was reflecting on this social reality one day nearly sixty years ago with Bernie Campbell, a neighbor and former schoolmate, as we were driving the hilly, dusty backroads of Lanark County, Ontario. "Well," Bernie said, "folks in the city have things we might wish we had. And they sure are stylish. But I ken what you say—a whole lot of them are too much like each other. What we have for neighbors out here is—well—more interesting. We have way more folks who are just themselves and nobody else." He pointed to a farm we were passing. "We sold a couple of heifers to that lad once." He launched into an exceptionally vivid recollection of a haggling session, concluding by saying, "Now *that* old lad, Davy-boy, was a *real character*."

That phrase, commonly used in our part of the world, may refer not only to an eccentric, but also to any person you wouldn't be likely to confuse with somebody else. I have chosen it as the title of this little book because it typically signifies a more or less consistently 'real' person, not a personage (or persona), one who acts and speaks pretty much exactly the same in public as in private. In a culture like that of the upper Ottawa Valley, in which stories about interesting people, living or dead, are a cherished form of entertainment around the stove in winter or the front porch in summer, there are many, many such "real character" stories. They form our oral history, and, though it might seem an irony, the telling of such stories about people who stand out from the herd in one way or another strengthens common identity among neighbors. We are—or used to be—a people who cherish odd-balls.

The Ottawa Valley is not, properly speaking a 'character' in this book, but sixty years ago it certainly *had* a unique character, and some of that still remains. Immigrant origin over nearly two centuries accounts for distinctive accents and tell-tale place names. From Hawkesbury seventy miles below Ottawa to Mattawa (both Algonquin names) more than one hundred miles north of it, settlement history came in three phases. The English came first, often from Yorkshire, yielding names such as Bytown (Ottawa's earlier name), Hull, across the river, Greely, Richmond, and the like. These are in the areas closest to Ottawa and were the first to be parceled out by agents of the Crown to settlers. Next came the Scots, mostly during the late 1700s through the first quarter of the next century, establishing to the south-east the counties of Stormont, Dundas, and Glengarry, then the counties of Lanark and Renfrew to the west and north-west. My mother's family and that of most of their kin came from the first area, my father's from the second, and I grew up in the area which extends through good farmland many miles from places like Kinburn, Arnprior, and Braeside until it bumps up against rough rock ridges and irregular hills of the Lanark Highlands near Burnstown, Calabogie, and Renfrew, before edging up and over the hills and following down the Tay River to Perth. By the time the poor Irish and Anglo-Irish came in the 1840s, all that was left was the rough country of Lanark and Renfrew counties. Like everyone else those folks were given a survey map, a bag of flour, a broad axe and other very basic supplies (for which they signed, as often as not, with an "X," being illiterate, unlike their Scottish neighbors) and then set out to clear, in their case, not only trees, but also rocks and boulders from their land. It was tough going. Such was the part of Lanark in which my father sought to establish his ranch. The land was rugged, and its people, both Scottish and Irish, like unto it. We long had a distinctive accent, a blend of Scottish and Anglo-Irish, which has attracted the interest of linguists. We preserved songs and fiddle tunes from the "auld sod" that made our cèilidhs and fairs as distinct as our tell-tale accent.

Though I propose to pay tribute in these pages to characters I met in other parts of the world—the United States, England and Italy as well—some of my own favorite "real characters" remain those I came to know when I was younger. Thus, my readers will note that a good many of the persons featured here are from the rural Ottawa Valley, a few from places a good way removed from it, but I think of them all as, in one way or another, "real characters." Each has an abiding place in my grateful memory because in some distinctive way that person challenged me, taught me, and helped keep my affectations in check. This does not necessarily mean, of course, that all were paragons of virtue.

Among country people there is a strong tendency to identify particular persons with what I like to call a "signature narrative." The concept is simple, but let me give a brief example.

One day I was walking through one of his back hayfields with Geordy Ellis, himself most definitely a "real character." We came to a stone fence, beyond which were substantial trees growing up in what apparently had once been meadows. There was a broken line of split cedar fence, disappearing ghost-like into the woods. Geordy saw me looking and said, "This stone one here is my line fence. That on the other side belonged to Jack Logan. It's long gone back to the Crown now, for taxes."

"Who was Jack Logan?" I asked, not having heard of him.

"One of the first here," said Geordy, "neighbor to my grandfather. No family."

He paused. "Let me tell you about Jack Logan. He was once called to be witness in the court at Almonte. It was a turkey thief had been caught. Judge said, 'Jack Logan, would you say that man over there was a turkey-stealer?' Jack thought a minute, then replied, 'Now Judge, you know I would not like to say such a thing

of any man.' And then, after a long pause: 'On the other hand. . .
if I was a turkey, and that lad was around, I'd roost me *real* high.'"

This brief story about Jack, still being told more than three
generations after his death, when his cabin and barn had long
become useless and his entire farm completely taken back by the
forest, remembered him for certain virtues. Apparently the stolen
turkeys were in fact his own, but there was in him no thirst for
revenge; he managed to bear witness to an obligated truth without risking false witness. His tact and prudential wisdom is still,
after all these years, offering counsel to those with ears to hear, not
least by means of a good laugh. There are other stories about Jack
Logan, but that one persists in community memory because it cap-
tures the character of the man, hence bears his 'signature'—even
though he was himself illiterate.

I want as much as possible to bear witness, by means of what
seem to me to be signature narratives, to people it has been my
privilege to know personally, unlike Jack Logan, who I know only
through Geordy's story.

Often those who tell such stories are as much a story as the
one of whom they speak. That would certainly be true of Geordy
Ellis. His six-hundred acre cattle farm, along the east shore of
White Lake and his famous and beautiful sugar bush, a magnifi-
cent stand of maples right by the road, earned him a meager living even after the one-room Uneeda school across the road had
been closed, and the students bussed away to the village of White
Lake, dispossessing Mrs. Ellis of a job. (Uneeda, by the way, got
its name from the whimsy of a late nineteenth-century bureaucrat
in some provincial department, who used a formula to determine
where rural post offices should be located. He had written 'uneeda
po here' on his map. There never had been more than the school,
Geordy's cabin, and the larger log house of his brother a mile up
the Bellamy Road, so the post office was fiction while the name remained—tenuously—a fact.) Geordy lived with his former school-
teacher wife, son, and daughter in their small log house—just a
cabin, really—with only one large downstairs room with a cook-
stove, table, chairs, and curtains to draw around the bed. There was

a small loft above for "the next generation." No indoor plumbing. Geordy had plenty enough money to build a bigger house. But he wouldn't. "Those townies," he once said to me, "spend money like water. This is all you really need," he said with a sweep of his arm at the old school house and his own cabin. "All you need, eh?" he repeated, with a laugh.

Geordy's brother Bill likewise had two children, a boy and a girl. The girl, Alice, had black hair, very white skin, and the biggest freckles I have ever seen. As soon as she graduated from high school she went off to get training as a nurse and never came back. The boy, who was named Elmer, didn't get past the first couple of grades in elementary school because he was 'mental,' as the family put it, probably afflicted with Down's syndrome or something like it. To keep him occupied, his father widened the peg hole on a big square barn timber (roughly 16 inches each side) about 12 feet long and ran a logging chain through it so Elmer could drag it up and down in front of the house. This pleased Elmer enormously, and over time he developed preternatural strength doing it. He had massive arms, hands, neck, and shoulders. Neighbors would marvel at his log-dragging, as it was called, but when he came to town with his father, to whom he was completely obedient, people greeted him affectionately. His favorite treat was a Dairy Queen cone, and that's where Arnprior folks would often encounter Bill and Elmer Ellis. Elmer spoke few words other than "g'day" or "thank you" and the like, but he smiled a lot and seemed content.

My father and I had firsthand experience of his strength. One day we were coming out the top of our lane in the old Fargo 2 ½ ton flat-bed we kept for hauling hay and feed. The Penishula Road, which runs off the Bellamy and out and down toward Pickerel Bay, is a bit blind just past the ranch lane because of the steep hill on the left, and what with the roar of our old Fargo Dad didn't hear the schoolbus coming, and we barely missed a crack-up by swinging hard right. Unfortunately, though the bus passed safely by, one set of our dual wheels was left in mid air over the ditch next to the culvert. Accordingly, we couldn't get traction to go either forward or back. Several minutes passed, and I was just about to walk the mile back and get the tractor and a chain when a faded blue Ford pick-up appeared.

"Trouble?" asked Bill Ellis. Dad explained. Bill got out of his truck and said simply, "Elmer can fix this."

He called Elmer over and showed him how we were hung up. Elmer grinned at us and said nothing, but got in the ditch, went into a kind of sumo-wrestler crouch with his hands under the back of the flat-bed and with a great grunt heaved it up on the road far enough that we had traction. I gasped something or other. Dad said, "that lad of your is some strong, Bill," and Elmer replied with a grin. We thanked them and they were off.

You don't forget a neighbor like that. Sadly, after his parents at last got to be frail and were worried that he might do harm, Elmer ended up in a provincial facility for the mentally challenged. It so happened that by the time he reached his late twenties he would occasionally speak to a woman, saying, "Nice lady," and try to pat her arm. Then he took to wandering—sometimes gone for two days. Once he showed up at our back door when neither Dad nor any of my brothers were around, and just stood out there saying "Nice lady." My mother was terrified, and locked herself in till Dad returned. By this time Elmer had wandered homeward, and Dad met him coming down the lane; he offered Elmer a ride home, and it was accepted. When Elmer was finally institutionalized, even though most neighbors could see it was probably necessary, the community was conflicted. "You have to see the sense in it," said Donald McNabb, "but all the same you hate to see it come to this." He spoke for many—though not my mother.

It is worth noting the circumstances leading to Elmer's being unable to live at home with his frail and aging parents, namely, the alarming reality of his strength as a danger, now, sixty-five years later, is not often retold, but the story of "how Elmer lifted Lyle Jeffrey's big Fargo truck out of the ditch with his bare hands" is one that remains; it has become his "signature" narrative, and many people besides members of my family tell it. Elmer may well—if oral history is not entirely extinguished by modern entertainments—be remembered as long as Jack Logan.

The persons you will meet in these pages include a cast of old neighbors, Ottawa Valley farmers, ranchers, a rodeo ringer, and other such folk, also a crazy nun, an English poet, and a wonderful auto mechanic. Each of them is one of the people I have come over time to appreciate as "real," people for whom private and public selves were largely identical, yet who marched to the beat of a different drummer than many of the rest of us. I am grateful to them all. If you enjoy some of these folks half as much as I do still, then writing these narratives down will have been worth it.

POP SHAVER

ALMOST EVERYONE CAN REMEMBER a teacher who wasn't insufferable. Maybe if you are lucky you even had one who made a difference. A few of us are thankful for a teacher who turned our lives around. In my case it was Bernard Shaver—"Pop" Shaver as he was universally known outside of class—a grade eight teacher whose specialty at Glashan Public School was unruly boys, lads with a penchant for too frequently exhibiting a surfeit of testosterone. All thirty-six of us in his 1952–53 class came trailing a litter of misdemeanor citations; neither our previous schools nor our parents had proven sufficient for our correction. We were segregated from the girls our age (mostly 12 and 13) for good reasons. I don't remember the name of their teacher, or the name of the one who taught the "normal" boys either. But I'll never forget Pop Shaver as long as I live.

He was already in his sixties, of middle height but with large, strong, bony hands. His face was creased, his nose also large, and there was sparkle in his eyes and sometimes fire. Yet he had a wonderful beaming smile that could as suddenly light up the classroom as his frown could shut it down; he had a gravelly voice that made him seem forever hoarse, as if he had once had a cold he never quite got over, but it was a voice you wanted to listen to—carefully. One of the students, a chap named Rich Little, could mimic Pop well enough that he would scare and scatter us when we were rolling dice for money in the school basement—so good was he in fact that one time it really *was* Pop calling down the stairs, and

1

I can attest that, believing it was just Rich, we did not scatter fast enough. That was not such a good day.

Pop taught us mathematics and English. We had classes in woodworking and metalwork to which we went twice weekly, and music appreciation once on Fridays. I remember the two shop teachers, Mr. Fraser and Mr. Castleman, but not the name of the music teacher, who was a bit of a twit and who, because I disliked opera, made me do my term paper on Puccini's *Madame Butterfly*. Social Studies, with the eminently distractable Mrs. MacDonald, we had gotten out of the way back in grade seven, so the only other non-Shaver class besides PE was French, for which an intern-instructor from the Normal School came to us, also twice a week. What this meant in sum is that from 8 to 11 a.m., before our one-hour 'other' classes, five days a week, Pop Shaver taught us math. He worked us hard, and we got good at it, much better than we knew until Pop came to class with first one, then two, then three of our tests that a friend of his had administered at Lisgar Collegiate to the graduation class, five years our seniors. (We had, by Christmas, significantly better scores.) The entirety of every afternoon was reserved for English.

It would not be too much to say, in my case, that these afternoons utterly transformed my life. I had been reading adult books avidly on my own for three or four years—Dickens, Scott, Eliot, de Maupassant, Hugo, and others. But I had never before had the experience of thoughtful, penetrating conversation about such books, or of questions that made you delve far more deeply into their thought. Pop was not just a sharp mathematician, but also a man of the text; as I can better see now, he was an acute reader with a prodigious memory, a supple imagination, and critical acumen. But he was also a man for contexts; he would tell us fascinating things about an author's life and times, historical events that swept over the author's horizon and still cast shadows on our own. He had a fine ear for irony, such as most twelve-year-old boys do not, and he would draw it out for us, often just by reading aloud brilliantly until he saw our lights come on. Then he would laugh, and exclaim, "Isn't it marvelous, lads?" We came to agree, then to anticipate. Not in the least afraid of morality, he would arrange texts so that in their succession in his syllabus (which we never got except as he announced it weekly) the connections would gradually dawn on us, setting him up for a deeper but pithy lesson. Thus, in the autumn we read (and learned to act out the parts of) Shakespeare's *Merchant of Venice*. The cruelty of Shylock in that play is overmatched by Portia's mercy, you may remember, but not many came to sympathize with Shylock. When in February we came to *Ivanhoe*, however, something different happened. The wounded Ivanhoe's life is saved by Isaac the Jew and his beautiful daughter Rebecca, who nurses him back to health. When at the denouement Ivanhoe is wedded to Rowena, as destiny demands, and Isaac and Rebecca sail to Granada to rejoin the Sephardic community, some of us were a bit disappointed. "How many of you were hoping he would marry Rebecca?" Some of us raised our hands. "Me too," he said with a smile and a wink. We weren't just plodding through texts.

We didn't immediately realize, of course, just how unusual our experience was. All we knew is that for the first time in our lives we weren't bored to death by school, and that when Pop was teaching he had our full attention. One day two young men appeared at the classroom door. Just as Pop went to greet them a message came from the principal's office that he was wanted on the phone, so he asked the young men to wait in the class till he returned. "Boys," he said to us, "these fellows are former students from this class who are now studying for their degrees at Cambridge, in England." He introduced them by name, and left. One of the boys came in and sat at his desk (Pop almost never sat there—he always taught standing or moving about); the other leaned with his rear on the top of the desk, facing us, and said, "I hope that you little thugs know what you've got here; maybe the best teacher in the world." The other said, "Without this man we'd be working in a lumber-yard or maybe in jail. He changed us. We just came back to thank him." For five minutes they let us ask questions about university life and about Cambridge. I don't think the idea of university had crossed many of our minds before—certainly not mine. Then Pop suddenly came back, cheerily asked the two some questions of his own, and with a pat on their shoulders saw them out the door. "Alright, boys, now for us it's back to work."

Pop's manner of discipline—the charism of his character and the awe he inspired without much raising his voice—were absent, of course, when he was not in the room. This was particularly so for our instruction in French, which at the beginning of my year was provided by a rather pretty but nervous Normal School student intern who came to our room twice a week. Pop would then leave her to it and take a break. We were not only lacking in comparable awe for this young apprentice, it would be fair to say that in her nervousness and good looks she brought out the worst in us. There was much twittering behind her back whenever she turned to write out a declension on the blackboard, which was often, as she clearly did not much like eye contact with a room full of rascals such as we were. As was my wont, I sat at the back of the room, in the middle, and one day, when she seemed particularly distracted, I am ashamed to say that I threw a small rubber eraser her way. It bounced off the blackboard and hit her on the shoulder; she immediately burst into tears and fled the room. In a minute the door opened again and Pop strode in. In less time than it takes me to tell it, he said, "Alright, everybody on their feet. Now, those who did not *see* this, sit down." Half the class, those to the front, sat. "Now everybody who did not *do* this, sit down." And there I was, standing alone. "Jeffrey, come with me." It was that quick. The strap was not more painful than my shame.

Pop had a concern for our developing a sense of proper courtesy toward women. He strongly supported our being taught to dance with girls, at some special Phys Ed classes. And he went out at recess with us to the rink, and taught us how to skate with girls, to the Vienna Waltz and other such music. I was very reluctant. "Here, Jeffrey, you stand right here beside Miss Bell. Now hold her left hand with yours, and put your right hand on the small of her back. Now both of you skate to the music." At first I was mortified; later, of course, I came to appreciate that he was teaching us the decorum appropriate to being young men of a better caliber than might have been foreseen.

Pop reinforced all this by teaching—and getting us to memorize—many poetic passages from the Old Testament, something no teacher today would be permitted to do. Psalm 1, 50, 100 and Ecclesiastes 12 were all on the spring term memorization and recitation schedule. I remember particularly the Ecclesiastes, "Remember now thy creator in the days of thy youth, while the evil days come not, nor the years draw nigh, when thou shalt say, 'I have no pleasure in them.'" He led us through that text with great care, asking many questions. "What do you think it means, boys, when it says 'and all the daughters of song are brought low; they are afraid also of what is high'?" That was quite a discussion—a class such as I have scarcely been able to match in fifty years of my own teaching. Many years later, the parish priest who would marry my wife and me told me quietly, "I had Pop Shaver just four years before you. He, more than anyone in seminary, taught me the meaning of the 'fear of the Lord.'" I laughed. Father Pat had been a rowdy, so I expected a funny tale, but no: "I loved that man so much that I was more than anything afraid to disappoint him." After a few months in his class, though with much less theological insight than Fr. Pat, I'd say that pretty much all of us felt the same way.

One thing that set Friday afternoons apart for us was recitation. Each week we were given a poem to memorize. At first they were shorter poems, such as Keats's sonnet, "On First Looking into Chapman's Homer." Pop would work through the poem for us, give us background information (we were astonished that the excitement of an explorer first glimpsing the Pacific could be compared to a reader's discovery of a translation of a Greek text), and then he would say, "Alright boys, that's for next Friday." We never knew who would be called upon to recite, just that it would be six of us, chosen at random. The issue was not whether or not you had the poem memorized (God help you if you didn't), but whether you could show, by your recitation, that you really understood it. Pop would make comments on the recitations overall, have a suggestion, then an admonition, then assign the next poem.

As the weeks went on the poems became noticeably longer: Tennyson's "Ulysses," Gray's "Elegy in a County Churchyard," Coleridge's "Ode to Tranquility," and then "Kubla Khan." By then, it was early November, and I remember being hard-pressed to show I really understood "Kubla Khan." I didn't. But then came the mimeographed copy of our next assignment—more than one hundred lines from Byron's "Childe Harold's Pilgrimage." Four pages. An audible groan was emitted by several voices (I stress that such utterances were not normally tolerated in Pop Shaver's class, and well we knew it.) But we were staggered by the length of this assignment. Pop just raised his eyebrow at us, stood silent for a minute, and then, in a total departure from his usual drill, offered no context whatsoever for the poem. Instead, he walked over to the window, and laid his hand on the frame. Outside it was raining—I can see it in my mind as if it were yesterday. He paused, then simply began to recite.

> There was a sound of revelry by night,
> And Belgium's capital had gathered then
> Her beauty and her chivalry, and bright
> The lamps shone o'er fair women and brave men.
> A thousand hearts beat happily; and when
> Music arose with its voluptuous swell,
> Soft eyes looked love to eyes which spake again,
> And all went merry as a marriage bell,
> But hush! hark! A deep sound strikes like a rising knell!
>
> Did ye not hear it?—No, 'twas but the wind,
> Or the car rattling o'er the stony street;
> On with the dance! Let joy be unconfined;
> No sleep till morn when youth and pleasure meet
> To chase the glowing hours with flying feet. . . .

We were mesmerized by the power of his recitation, slow, measured, catching the rhythm of Byron's verse perfectly without overdoing it (as now I know). The opening roar of the cannons were real enough for us to feel the alarm:

> Within a windowed niche of that high hall
> Sate Brunswick's fated chieftain; he did hear

That sound the first amidst the festival,
And caught its tone with death's prophetic ear;
And when they smiled because he deemed it near,
His heart more truly knew that peal too well
Which stretched his father on a bloody bier
And roused the vengeance blood alone could quell:
He rushed into the field, and foremost fighting, fell.

For boys our age just seven years after the end of WWII, in which most of our fathers had fought, the story line was gripping. Byron goes on to describe in sharp detail the "sudden partings, such as press / The life from out young hearts," the mustering squadrons and the heavy thunder of advancing enemy artillery, the skirl and scree of the bagpipes, as "Wild and high the 'Camerons gathering' rose, / The war-note of Lochiel." But then, in a masterful shift in tone Byron touches upon the young troops themselves, heading out at dawn to the field.

And Ardennes waves above them her green leaves,
Dewy with Nature's tear-drops, as they pass,
Grieving, if aught inanimate e'er grieves,
Over the unreturning brave,—alas!
Ere evening to be trodden like the grass
Which now beneath them, but above shall grow
In its next verdure, when this fiery mass
Of living valour, rolling on the foe,
And burning with high hope, shall moulder cold and low.

He went on through the gory stanzas, past the reference to Psalm 90 in which "the Psalmist numbered out the years of man." And when he had finished, he paused a good minute in silence, and then turned to us and just said, "Friday, boys. Class dismissed." As we gathered our binders, we avoided eye contact with each other, for there was hardly a dry eye in the place. Some thugs. When the next Friday came, we were all wearing our five-cent plastic red poppies, as was Pop; it was November 11, and still raining. Even before the first boy was called up to recite, we had gotten the message.

Occasionally, in later life, boys from our class would chance to meet, and on recognition, spontaneously we'd exclaim together,

"There was a sound of revelry by night!" And like as not, look for a pub, there to reminisce about Pop Shaver. None of us that I know has ever had a teacher like unto him. For us he was, simply, the best teacher in the world.

Today, of course, he wouldn't be permitted to do most of what he did so well—in fact, he might not be permitted to teach at all in a public school. In an age that has reduced expectations to the infantilism of the 'Common Core,' indeed which seeks to deal palliatively rather than reconstructively with socially and emotionally challenged kids, he might well be regarded by progressive educationists as positively dangerous. Yet to all such prejudices I would offer a modest rejoinder: why not permit an experiment? If you can find such a teacher, even if one in a hundred, why not permit that teacher to design a curriculum that will challenge kids, move them out of and beyond their cultural norms, and let that good teacher freely teach to their full potential? Then, every five years for the next two decades, use *those* students as a control group when the success of the general population is assessed. I am willing to wager that the results might encourage us to give more attention to what makes for a good teacher, and less to rigid method and a curriculum whose purpose is mere social paradigm.

OLD JACK

OLD JACK BOX LIVED his whole life in a log house on the Penishula Road, west of Loney Lake on the way to Pickerel Bay. It was a subsistence farm, and Old Jack supplemented the family income by logging off mature pines and hardwood on their holdings.

Jack would have been close to eighty the year he came to our place with his "team and tools," as he called his mixed-breed horses and horse-drawn equipment. Dad had decided to take what hay he could off the lower forty acres nearest the lake and surrounding our house, all of it land too rough and rocky to risk modern machinery on. It would be both the first and last time for me to hay in the old way, but Jack had been doing it that way all of his life; some of the rusty equipment was his father's.

Jack began with the mowing, seated on his side-bar mower as it was pulled by the oldest of his two mares. Things went pretty smoothly, Jack stopping every hour or so to rest the mare and oil the squeaky mower. After that he waited for two days for the hay to dry before returning, this time with his team drawing a buck-rake behind. An advantage of this old way of doing things, especially over rough ground, is that thin patches and thick patches are less a problem; you just drive the horses until the rake has a full jag, then lock and drag it to where the coils are to be built. By the afternoon there were several of these jags grouped in each of the fields. That's when I was able to help, forking the jags into a coil, gradually building the stook, or pile, to cure. Curing took another two days.

It was late morning the day following when Jack arrived with team and wagon. We began immediately to fork hay up, working from stook to stook until we had a load. When we needed to move to the next stook, Jack would just say "Up" in a low voice, and the team would move forward till he said "Whoa," with him never needing to get up front and take the reins. It was as if his team knew what he was thinking. Once loaded too high for me to add more, off we'd go to the barn, there to fork the load into one side or other of the loft. Hot work it was, and during it all Jack said little. We'd let the horses drink, have some water ourselves, then go back for another load.

Finally, just as the sun was sinking behind the pines on the far side of the lake, and with only a last little bit of hay on our last load, Jack said "Steady" and the team stopped. Not sure why, I waited. Jack leaned against the wagon. The air was still, and as often happens on that lake in such an evening, the loons began to call, "laughing" as we say.

"I love to hear the loons at evening," said Jack. Then he added, "We say they laugh, but their song is sad."

I nodded.

"It's beautiful, but it makes me feel a wee bit lonely all the same," said Jack. I thought about asking why, then thought better of it. After a minute or so of quietness and an occasional loon call, Jack suddenly spoke again:

> O, reason not the need! Our basest beggars
> are in the poorest thing superfluous.
> Allow not nature more than nature needs,
> Man's life's as cheap as beast's.

"That sounds like poetry," I said.

"Well it is, or something like," Jack replied. "It's Shakespeare wrote it—in a play."

"I don't think I ever read that," I replied.

"No, it's not likely you would," said Jack. "It's *King Lear*. You are much too young for it."

"Our Shakespeare at Arnprior High School was just *Julius Caesar, Othello,* and *Midsummer Night's Dream.* We have *Henry IV* next year. What year of school did you read that in?"

"Not school, lad," he said slowly. "I had to leave school after grade six, to help at home. We have a Shakespeare in the house. Sits by the Bible. Sometimes after dinner I take a mood and read some. There's a lot I miss in it, but he's a great one to make you think."

Often over the years since, remembering that sunset conversation, it has come to me to add, as I did not then, "And so were you, Jack Box." I had, of course, to look up those lines to find them, and to wonder why he had them memorized. Sadly, there never came a time when I could ask him.

RUSSELL COMBA

RUSSELL WAS A LEAN man, with long arms, large hands, and a happy face. His ready smile and gentle, gracious manner made him welcome anywhere, but during the years I knew him best he lived alone. His father had died some years before; he stayed to help his mother until she also died. By then he was in his later fifties. He kept a clean house, was always neat even in work clothes; his trousers, held up by his father's leather suspenders, were neither stained nor torn, and when he dressed up and went to town on Friday evenings it was in his Sunday best. He would have a meal at Mosko's restaurant, chat with folks he knew for a while, then come home. Always willing to lend a hand, always cheerful, he was everyone's favorite bachelor.

One of my brothers and I asked him why he had never married. I was seventeen or eighteen at the time.

"Well, lads," he smiled, looking down at his well-oiled boots, "it's been a bit like this. Supposing you were walking through the bush, and it came to mind that you might see a good, smooth sapling such as would make for a fine walking stick. You see one that looks pretty good, but you think—no, I'll walk on a ways and maybe find a better one. Might be that this happens again. Then, the first thing you know, you're out of the bush."

He chuckled, "It'll be right enough for me as it is now. I'm pretty much accustomed to my life."

WILD BILL

It was the summer I turned fifteen that I really got to know our neighbor Bill Miller, aka "Wild Bill." That was what everybody called him, mostly in mild amusement, some perhaps with a hint of disdain in their voices. Bill was a son of Ernie and Sarah Miller, and had grown up to raising cattle, mixed farming, with some trapping and hunting on the side. Though the details always remained sketchy to me, he had a falling out with his brother that involved some kind of violence and trouble with the law. What I do know is that Bill didn't stick around for the proceedings but jumped in his pickup truck with his best horse in a trailer behind and headed west to try his luck on the rodeo circuit. When he returned he had perfected his skills as a heel-roper—none better to have around when a bull came up lame on the pasture and needed treatment. He was always a bit of a rough diamond, sure enough, but mostly reliable and a real good neighbor.

It seems that for three or four years he did just well enough to keep body and soul together; he was always as skinny as Slim Pickins in the Ace cartoons my dad liked to tack up on the corkboard beside his desk—but apparently doing horse, rope, and gun tricks paid some of his way. Eventually he came back, took over his uncle's farm/ranch and small log house almost directly opposite his folks' place. He had different horses now, one a paint stallion named Leo. Only Bill could ride him; he was a maverick through and through. Bill hired Leo out to stud, but you had to get your mare to Wild Bill's place if there was to be a transaction.

13

That was the context in which I got to know Bill better. Dad had some dealings with him, and he had been in our house once or twice (my mother was appalled by his unkempt appearance), but those situations were fleeting, if cordial. Bill laughed a lot—an odd laugh, half snort. He had a thin, reedy voice and was full of lore. Dad liked him as much as Mother didn't; he also liked paint horses. Soon we were taking mares to Bill's place to be bred. That's how one June morning I saddled Flicka, our red and white paint mare, to ride the seven miles to Bill's spread, as he liked to call it.

You might not think of horses as capable of passion, but you would be wrong. When Flicka was in heat, she was more hot to trot than trot could satisfy. We galloped almost the whole way, and when I got down to open Bill's gate she was foamy wet and so eager (she had been on the same errand there last year) that I could hardly remount before she was back at the gallop up Bill's nearly mile-long lane. When I pulled her up in front of the old log cabin, Leo was neighing and snorting loudly in the back corral. He knew.

Bill appeared on the porch, a glint in his coal-black eyes. "Well if it isn't Lyle's lad Dave—and Flicka, I see. Here for business?"

I acknowledged as much, swung down and took saddle, wet blanket, and bridle off Flicka. Bill had to get hold of Leo and hang on whilst I got Flicka to the corral gate. She popped inside like a flash, and with much squealing and nipping they went unceremoniously about the business at hand. We watched; it didn't take long.

"Come on back to the porch," said Bill. "They're not satisfied. We need to leave them for a bit. Here, put that wet saddle blanket on the rail here—no, upside down, so it dries some."

Instead of chairs on that porch, there were two sizable stumps. We sat. Across the lane on the roof of a cedar-shingled hay barn there was a very large hide staked out, flay-side up, drying in the sun. Sensing me look, Bill said, "Salted that bugger and put him up to dry day before yesterday. Black bear. Shot him over by the river, eating one of the beavers right out my trap."

"What are you going to do with it?" I asked.

"Make a rug," replied Bill. "Gotta cozy this place up for a woman coming."

Now, Bill's wife had left him long enough before that I never met her, and their three kids, William, Ronny, and Donna, were being raised across the road by Ernie and Sarah. It can be hard to know what to say next in such a situation, but I foolishly asked, ". . . a relative?"

He laughed. "Not yet, lad, and maybe never. But I could use a woman around here and I've been thinking of ordering one up from the *Family Herald*" (pronounced "famly hurled" in our neck of the woods).

"Order one up?" I was incredulous.

"Sure. Have you never seen the ads in the back of the *Herald*?"

Bill went into the house and soon returned with a copy of the old farm and ranch weekly, now long since defunct. He opened it to the want ads section and put his bony finger next to an entry which read "Good women interested in marriage to steady rural men. Apply for information."

"So I got me the catalogue," said Bill. "Come by the mail last week. Would you like to have a look, now?"

Curiosity was sufficient reason to reply in the affirmative and, after another quick turn in and out of his domicile, Bill emerged with a semi-gloss set of pages, each with half a dozen black and white photographs, with words underneath. Age, height, address.

"Just look at these, Dave," exclaimed Bill. "What do you think of that one, eh?" He grinned. "I'm thinking of ordering her up for to see if I like her. That's part of the deal. They come for a look-see, stay a day—or up to a week. Experimental-like."

I was beginning to sense the probability of paternal questions I didn't want to answer, so made an excuse to fetch Flicka (easier said than done, since Leo was still all worked up). I saddled up and wished Bill well with his experiment. As I cantered down the road past Lawson and Sadie Miller's place, whose house and barns were visible from the road, Lawson and Sadie were working their vegetable garden up with their old bay mare and cultivator. We waved at each other, but I did not stop till I was unsaddling Flicka back in our own corral.

"Everything go alright?" asked my father at supper.

"With Flicka."

"Problems?"

"Not really." I paused. "Is it really possible to order up a woman from the *Family Herald*?"

"Mail order brides," snapped my mother. "Absolutely horrible. It should have been outlawed years ago."

"It was common enough a generation ago," Dad said. "The government supported it for sparsely populated rural areas. But where did you come across this information now?"

"Bill," I said, "tells me he is ordering up one for experimental purposes."

"What?" exclaimed my mother. "What woman in her right mind would ever want to live with a man like that? In a place like that?"

"He's fixing it up."

"How?" asked my mother.

"He shot a bear, and is turning it into a rug."

A couple of weeks later I rode in Bill's lane again, on Sundance, a sorrel mare who showed herself to be in season but, as the biting, kicking and squealing in Leo's corral well demonstrated, was considerably less eager than Flicka. We were concerned things might get out of hand and so waited by the corral for quite a while. The job got done, but I doubt there was much satisfaction in it, either for Leo or our mare. She had quite a few chunks out of her hide when I came to saddling her up for the ride home.

That's when I noticed the woman on the porch. She was short, thin, and had dark hair. Bill didn't offer to introduce us, so I bid him goodbye and rode out.

It was at least three weeks before I came back to Bill's—mid-July already—with Birdie, a sixteen-and-a-half hand red and white paint cutting horse, the last mare Dad wanted to settle to Leo, Bill's stallion. When I got to the house Bill had heard me coming and he was on the porch to greet me. So was somebody else.

"Well, David, this here is Phil. Phil, this is Lyle's lad I tolt you about." Bill was obviously in a high mood. Phyllis McCullogh, as her full name turned out to be, was a large, big-framed girl with very white skin, open features, blue eyes and light brown hair. She simply said, "Pleased to meet you," with a shy smile. She was dressed in denim overalls.

Bill and I went about the business that brought me.

"Well, what d'you think? Seems okay, don't she? Only seventeen. Very strong, but peaceable-like. She comes from a famous family. Scotch Lake, New Brunswick." Bill was speaking even more rapidly than normal. "Sir Charles Tupper was one of her ancestors."

"I thought you said she came from the *Family Herald?*"

"Yep. Sure did. Had to try two others before I hit on her. Third time's the charm, lad. Those other two were awful. With one of them I had to hide the burdizzo."

I laughed. "Well, this one's pretty young, Bill."

"Best way," he cut in. "Get 'em young and raise 'em up to your own liking. And hey, come have a look here at what she brought with her."

We walked around behind a smaller outbuilding, attached to which was a small log-built pen.

"Look at that, Dave." Bill pointed to a large, white heifer, munching on some hay in the feeder. "Ever seen one of them before?"

I hadn't. Beef cattle in our parts were either "white-faced" (Herefords) or "baldies" (Angus-Hereford cross). Dad's cousins, the Donaldsons by Cedar Hill, had dual purpose Durham Shorthorns, but they were getting to be few and far between.

"That there is a French breed," said Bill proudly. "They call them Charly."

It would be some time before I would see more Charolais. They were just being introduced to North America, in the then fashionable quest for larger beef animals.

"That heifer come in a cattle car back of the same train as brought her—far as Smith's Falls. Present from her father. She calls it 'half her dowry.' If I treat her right and get properly married and all, we just have to send her father a copy of the certificate and he'll send us another Charly heifer to keep the first one company."

17

It took till November three years later before the knot had been officially tied, and the second heifer arrived later in the month. I had to admit that they were a handsome pair.

I have also to admit that Bill and Phil went on to have what to all appearances was a reasonably happy marriage. We have a saying that "strong women make good husbands" and maybe some of that applied. She took over care of the cattle and added a Guernsey milk cow for the sake of the kitchen. Bill told me later that she would have preferred a Jersey, a breed he described as only fit for "someone too poor to own a cow and too proud to keep a goat." Phil also acquired some goats, chickens, and (less successfully) a few sheep. They had a son when she was twenty-one and he was forty-two. They named him John, and he grew to have hair like his mother's and her blue eyes too.

There are far more Wild Bill stories than I can tell here. He taught me a few tricks with horses, for which I was grateful. He also got me to assist him in throwing colts, so he could 'cut them,' for which I was not so grateful. After I went to university I saw him only on summer holidays occasionally, but during my first year teaching (1968) my stories about him got the attention of a colleague of mine, Paddy Grant. Paddy was from Northern Ireland. We were heading back to Victoria together from research trips the following summer, and he asked if we could come by way of the Ottawa Valley so he could see some of it for himself. Thus it was that one fine afternoon in late August I drove into Bill's laneway with Paddy aboard.

Bill greeted me at the gate and let us in. As we walked toward their new house, a bungalow nearer the road to replace the log house which had burned three winters before, Bill stopped to snatch the slingshot from young John's hand.

"That's not how I learnt yeh," he snapped, then quick as a striking snake fired two stones at John's tin can target, hitting it both times and sending it flying. He flung the slingshot down at John's feet and said, "*That's* how I learnt yeh." Bill was a crack shot with a rifle too—I've seen him hit five bottle caps in a row off a fence rail at fifty yards, quick as he could crank the lever of his .30–30 Winchester.

Paddy rolled his eyes at me as we followed Bill to the front door, where Phyllis was standing with her usual grin.

"Come on in," she said, after introductions. "I hope you will stay for supper. I have a roast in the oven and potatoes. Lots enough to go around."

I looked at Paddy. He indicated agreement, so we were there a while. With his hat off I noticed that Bill was losing his hair quite rapidly. He was as much of a talker as ever, though, and he regaled us with yarns about one thing or another. He pointed to the large mural of a black and white pinto, painted right onto the sheetrock wall of the main room. "Leo," he said. "Gone now. Went out one morning to feed him and there he was, down and out. Kept his hide, though."

He pointed to two overstuffed chairs covered with black and white horse hide. He laughed.

"Couldn't let him go altogether," he said.

"By the way, Phil has new teeth!" Bill exclaimed. "C'mon, Phil, show the lads your teeth."

Phyllis, shy enough still, smiled but demurred.

"C'mon, Phil," said Bill, leaping up and grasping her by the lower and upper lip as you would a horse, baring her dentures. "Cost a damn fortune," Bill said. "But they make her happy, even if she is shy about showing them."

Wishing for her sake to change the subject I asked him how his trapping had gone last winter. "Lots of beaver," he said, "some muskrat. But the fur isn't worth much anymore. What I trap the beavers for is mainly the testicles."

"The testicles?" Paddy sputtered. I knew he didn't believe it. So did Bill. He looked at Paddy square in the eye and said, "So why don't you come down to the basement and have a look for yourselves?" He was including me for politeness, but I waved Paddy on by himself.

"What use are beaver testicles?" asked the incredulous Paddy.

"Perfume," replied our host. "I've got four hundred pair nailed up around the basement to cure. The buyer will come for them in September." When Paddy emerged from the basement with Bill behind, grinning, his Irish face was pale and he was blinking his eyes.

We ate the food that was set before us, sparing not for conscience sake, as the apostle recommends. The roast and mash was followed by quite good apple pie with cheddar cheese on the side.

"How's your father?" Bill asked.

"Okay," I answered.

"Same age as me and Billy Graham," Bill informed Paddy. "Lyle always tried to get me to take up religion. Gave me a little book by Billy Graham. It was interesting, but I have objections."

Paddy, always more interested in objections than affirmations, perked up. "What objections, if you don't mind?"

"Well, to begin with, Noah. I simply can't see why he wouldn't have squashed them pairs of mosquitoes, black flies, deer flies, and the like when he had the chance."

We all laughed.

"So they are a local manifestation of the problem of evil?" Paddy laughed, but he was foolishly playing the professor.

"I don't know about that," said Bill, "but if you came back here in May you'll wish he had squashed all those pairs of devils when he had the chance. Lyle says they leave bites as bad as emerods."

"Emerods?" asked Paddy.

"There's a town near here called Ashdad," I said.

"Ashdad?" Paddy queried again.

"Ashdad. Look it up."

Phyllis lived only to about the age of fifty-four. Bill lived on a few years longer, but in considerable dejection. He got to watching television. My brother Dale once encountered him in the Centennial Restaurant in Pakenham, looking pretty wan, having coffee and pie with a couple of men Dale didn't know. He was wearing a curly orange wig. Dale asked him, "What's with the wig, Bill?"

"My bald head was getting so damn cold in winter, even with a cap. Ordered two for the price of one from a magazine. The one with black hair didn't fit."

Dale didn't know what to believe, but he told me later, "Bill looked like Bozo the Clown without the makeup. What a sad way to wind down for a real character like Bill."

I prefer to remember Bill in his prime, that day he introduced me to his mail-order bride.

SADIE AND LAWSON

I. The Advent of Sadie Miller

We were always great ones to cut wood,
not that we ever needed it. Sure,
we often had it years ahead of ourselves.
Never mind. It was work we did together.

So there we were, moving along the road,
with axe and the chainsaw, humming.
"Lawson," I said, "who could think of a better time?"
"Time is what you make it," he said, pulling the saw cord.
"And I've made a lot of it," I told him
into the noise. He didn't hear.

At sixteen married.
Forty-five years: him—our children—theirs.
And Lord knows how many hundred cords of wood.
Trees: felled, limbed, cut, split, stacked,
burning. Brush and woodlot full of our talk
as then gone drifting off in smoke
now lured to ground again—
new trees, like shaggy spears.

"So help me steady. This," he said,
as drawing me close to the greying trunk,
"I've trouble with the burl."
But hardly my hands were there
than under, the blade began to twist,
and in a last slow tearing

turned with a terrible snap
and knocked me down
to sleep.

So, let me leave you, then, with this:
If anyone says, "she never knew"
they'll know nothing of what they say.
Though I couldn't feel his hands,
I knew him there, could hear
in the wind his frightened pleas
and saw at the last myself and him—floating
above us, my body and man, saw there
that road and bush, the house
and one last line of spinning smoke
gone from the kitchen stove.

Then came the light:
the splendid, lovely light. . . .

II. At Sadie Miller's Wake

At first we groped in the dark
for words, numbed by the shock.

In the night, when walls fall in
and we lie trapped below
what might be miles of rock
it's all too much at once—
thoughts break.

But if, when the bones unfold
the silence fills our ears,
each cavity, our very veins,
and we hear one other breathing—
Be sure of it.

We will speak:
talk reverently of harvest,
of sunlight and the evening hours
when men should rest
and the whole world change.

III. Lawson Miller's Christmas

Stooped in the thick of an empty gloom
nothing appears, no speaking stills my fears
and all I am climbs rough, hunched,
at the roof of my mouth, throat clogged
like a choking gall: this refuse, this desire.

Where is she now, what other place?
Here, in the grey of snow and tree-wreathed
Christmas sky
I've walked beyond the gleam
far past the stars that lit, at least, the thought.
Night and the New Year come; the old hours pass
like icicles along that path, edge-melt and breaking off,
falling and swallowed up in an unforgiving thaw.

The knot is done. I stand this beam alone.
No living thing to meet me, reach the place
and worse, I cannot dream her face
can't put my arm around her shoulder,
taste her tears against my own.

Why do I think that she is crying, there?
Why does it seem that she is crying too?

Lord have mercy
    on her tears
Christ have mercy
    on my fears
Lord have mercy

WILLARD CAMPBELL

I FIRST MET WILLARD Campbell in McLoughlins' General Store in the summer of 1957. I had just obtained my driver's license and was filling up my A49 Austin so that I could make it to Arnprior and back to the ranch later that evening.

Folks would regularly congregate in "the White Lake store," as it was also called, since it was on the corner opposite the church and equally friendly. Several locals were chatting when I came in to lay my five-dollar bill on the counter, and one of them—I think Buddy Lyndsay—said to a round-faced man coming in just after me, "G'day Willard. We haven't seen you in a long time, not even at church."

I would later learn that Willard was reclusive, a grade-school dropout and, though not entirely anti-social, certainly on the Asperger's spectrum somewhere. But he was, as it proved, always cheerful.

"Now Buddy, don't be getting preachy on me," Willard replied. "The Sabbath was made for man, not man for the Sabbath."

Everyone laughed.

Then Willard fixed his eye on me and said, "Now you'd be the oldest Jeffrey lad, wouldn't you? David, right?" It turned out that he had learned as much when Dad and I came to their place to buy a load of alfalfa hay for our horses. He had noticed and remembered me, whilst I had noticed only the voice of a man up in the mow, the reclusive Campbell brother, obscured by shadow and dust, throwing down bales faster than I could stack them. His brother Dougall took the money, and I didn't see Willard come down.

I acknowledged my identity.

"Well, David, you'd be 16 years old, I'm guessing last June, and you weigh 170 pounds."

"How would you know that?" I asked. Willard just grinned. "Oh, I know," he said.

Laughter from everyone. Then Donald McNabb said, with a twinkle in his eye, "He not only knows, but he wins prizes at the fair for guessing people's weights within two pounds."

Then I remembered that I had seen him at a kiosk doing just that at the Arnprior Fair. And I knew myself to be about 170 pounds.

"How do you do that?" I asked.

"My secret," replied Willard. "Now what day in June would your birthday be, lad?"

I told him.

"And he'll never forget it," added Jimmy McLoughlin. "You'll see."

Willard and I didn't cross paths much, despite our proximity, especially after I went off to university the next year. In fact, I'm not sure if I even saw him once until more than twenty years later. I was with a west coast friend, and we were waiting by the Inner Harbor Bus Station in Victoria for the ferry bus to empty so that we could get on. Suddenly I heard a voice, and looked up to see a beaming Willard Campbell, stepping down from the bus.

"Why hello, David Jeffrey," he said in his cheery, sing-song voice. "Your birthday is June 28, 1941 and you now weigh just about 212 pounds."

"Willard Campbell!" I exclaimed. "What brings you here?"

"Same as yourself, most likely!" he replied. "I always wanted to see this beautiful place, so one day I just got on a bus and headed west."

My friend and I had to get ourselves on the bus, so I just said, "You are an amazing fellow, Willard Campbell," as I climbed up the steps. When I looked out the window he was waving at me.

My friend was stupefied. "Who was that?"

It isn't easy to explain such a person to someone who hasn't grown up in our neck of the woods, but I tried.

NICK AND JIM

IN SOME PEOPLE DISTINCTIVE character seems to reveal itself most clearly in interaction with another individual. This was the case with Jim Wright. To get the full measure of the man you had to see him reacting to Nick. Nick was a timber wolf.

Jim came to work for us in "The Luggage," as locals called the small leather goods factory my father started. It served mostly to defray losses incurred by our ranch, whether in cattle, horses, or in the summer riding camp my folks ran for more than twenty years. Jim had worked with horses, logging in the north, and came to know my father through a group called the Shantymen's Association. These were a hardy lot, mostly loggers but also miners and prospectors. Jim had a stint as a prospector too—scouting possible sites for mining companies, spending weeks at a time traversing the roadless wilderness. He had seen a lot and, though gentle in spirit, was tough as ironwood.

Jim was a burly man, with a nearly 19-inch neck, shoulders like an NFL tackle's, and hands strong enough that he casually cracked the walnuts in his lunch without the aid of a nutcracker. He had sparkling blue eyes behind his thick glasses, and astigmatism in one eye that made you think he was looking behind you as well as at you all at once. He had a laugh all his own, and it could be heard a long ways off. Partly because he was our shipper, assembling orders for pickup, he was in many ways more a presence in the local community than my father, and he was certainly everyone's favorite fellow-worker at the shop. He was an elder in a small Plymouth Brethren chapel, and though he made little obvious effort to persuade 'outside' people to attend, he was a strong spiritual presence in the lives of almost everybody who knew him, including me. I knew his three children and was aware that he read to them from a large family Bible after each evening meal, and aware too that they affirmed the custom. "He has been to me far more kindly a priest than the one at our Church," said one of the Catholics who worked with us. I remember my father referring to Jim appreciatively as our "shop chaplain." Ellard Farrell, the rascally and very comical Irishman who brought snacks at break-times and lunch, spoke for many when he said at Jim's graveside, "I don't know if there is a heaven or not, but if there is, that's where Jim is right now." Jim Wright was a light for many and a rock for some.

After the factory had been broken into three times in three months, each time losing us expensive office equipment mostly, Jim said to Dad, "You need to get a big watchdog. German Shepherd maybe." Dad thought that a good idea, so he sent me to the Humane Society down in Ottawa to see what I could find. What I found was Nick.

In those days it wasn't unusual to go into the cage area at the Humane Society and see a fawn, even a bear cub, gathered up unwisely by people who saw them alone by the road and 'rescued' them. Though disapproving of this well-intended activity, the staff had large pens for such animals until they could find a zoo willing to adopt them. This time, after I was admitted to the pen area, I was astonished to see a young timber wolf pacing like a tiger up and down the length of a large pen. He had a thick grey coat and amber-green eyes. I was fascinated.

When I asked the keeper, he said, "That poor fellow will be euthanized tomorrow."

"That would be a terrible," I replied. "Why not just release him back into the woods north of Gatineau Park?"

"Can't be done," the keeper said. "He's been half a pet since he was a pup. Brought in here by the little old lady who had him since her son brought him back from the DEW line up north. Seems her son found a litter and saved this one. Brought it down for his mother to raise, but after about five months it started dragging her face-down on the sidewalk when she took him out. Must weigh eighty, maybe ninety pounds already—almost as much as herself. She tried to get her brother to take it on his farm out by North Gower, but while they were talking about it this guy pulled free of her and leapt over a pretty high mesh-wire fence into the chicken yard and killed a couple dozen quick as I just said it. That's when she gave up and brought it here."

I was watching the "half a pet" all the while, as he continued pacing swiftly up and down.

"How about I adopt him?" I blurted out. "I came here to get a big watchdog and he'd be all of that and more." I explained our situation, including my own background with training dogs and horses, and offered to take personal responsibility. The keeper was skeptical, but he clearly didn't want to euthanize this beautiful specimen either.

Neither, it turned out, did his boss, whom he consulted. It was decided—as never could happen now—that if I signed papers assuming complete liability should trouble arise, I could take him home. I was twenty-one. I signed.

Dad was astonished when I drove up to the plant with Nick in the back of our 1955 Plymouth station wagon. I had put the seats down flat to give him room, and he had been moving about rambunctiously the whole way back from Ottawa. The car was a mess, the windows all smeared and steamed up. When I walked him into the warehouse he nearly pulled me over.

Dad said, "That's not a dog."

I made my case as best I could. The idea that I had assumed *personal* legal responsibility for "the beast," as my father referred to him, relieved him some, but he warned me, "You may have signed your life away."

The plan was to keep him in the factory at night. During the day he would be chained to a dump trailer filled with gravel. After a week I went out to bring him in for the night and he was gone; he had broken a half-inch steel chain. I panicked, figuring there was nothing to do but take the wagon and go looking. Just then Dad got a call from Lyle Smith, a second cousin of Dad's who ran the Dairy Queen up on the highway, half a mile away.

"I've got your wolf here," Lyle said, "and he is front paws up on my counter. I am feeding him ice cream cones to keep him occupied. He likes them a lot, but you'd better come quick because all my customers are locked into their cars, terrified."

Sure enough. I got Nick into the wagon and settled my considerable bill with Lyle Smith. Afterward, whenever he escaped either by breaking his chain or, after I had a half-acre frost-fence pen right behind the plant built for him, just by jumping the seven-foot fence, he would head straight for the Dairy Queen. I reckon that his first owner, the old lady, must have taken him to a similar place for treats as a small pup.

By later in the fall, with cooler weather, Nick changed his tactics. Instead of heading to the Dairy Queen he would just run like the wind down one road after another. The only way to catch him was to get parallel to him, at 45 miles an hour, then move slightly ahead with the back of the Plymouth open. He loved to jump right in at that speed, and if there was meat for him to eat, I could usually slip on his choker chain and leash after he inhaled it and snub that to the steering wheel once I got stopped, and that would give me time to get out and close the rear hatch.

Nick got the back of that Plymouth pretty well scuffed up, one day especially. We drove past a German Shepherd who ran after us, barking. Nick didn't bark, but he nearly tore his way through the back hatch to get at him. Later that same day I was taking him out to the ranch to give him, as I fancied, a walk in the wild. Except for that German Shepherd he never paid the slightest attention to other dogs, or even cats. But as we drove down the lane past one of our pastures that had some yearling heifers on it he nearly tore through the side of the wagon right behind me. Again, no sound, but such determination as rocked the Plymouth from side to side. He was frantic to get one of those heifers for himself.

Life with Nick was beginning to become hectic as well as worrisome. The local police chief made us put up a sign outside the shop saying "These premises patrolled by a wolf. Does not bark or growl before striking." And there was an internal warning—from Jim.

At first Jim had said simply, "You have taken on more than you can handle." Then he began to tell stories of people he knew who suddenly had been attacked and killed by a timber wolf they thought was their pet. I protested that Nick was "taming," that I could handle him, even though I knew he was like no dog I had ever had. Those amber green eyes never quite met mine. No acknowledgment. He seemed to look right through me. He didn't care one way or another about being petted, though he was plenty glad to see me when I brought him his daily meal—anywhere up to 12 pounds of raw beef, though usually 5–6. We had an agreement with the Arnprior kill-plant butcher, who often had spoiled meat from canners and cutters, and saved me fifty or sixty pounds of spoilt meat each week in a box. Nick was growing fast; soon his head was at my belt level, and on the shipping scale he was 145 pounds. Jim said, "If he wanted to kill you, lad, it would be over before you saw it coming."

I was resistant even so. For one thing, the break-ins had stopped. The *Arnprior Chronicle* had a photographer come out and take a picture. Nick took a disliking to the man, and the photo showed him at the end of his chain lunging toward the camera. They printed that photo on the front page of the paper along with the police warning we were required to post on the front of the building. One night the constable found a back door slightly ajar; he refused to go in and called me instead. Now to get to the main power switch it was necessary to walk through the front office, another fifteen paces or so, then turn to the right into the shipping room, work your way along the back wall till you found the switch, and throw it. When I did, I turned around to see Nick standing silently behind me. He had followed me but his walking made no noise. It made me pretty thoughtful.

The next day Jim called me to his desk and said, "Come and see something you need to know."

Well, by this time we knew that our seven-foot fence couldn't keep Nick in, so Jim had gotten a big iron bar, had the blacksmith weld a heavy iron ring near the top of it, and with his own 25 pound sledge hammer had driven the rod nearly three feet down into a crevice in the limestone rock. Henceforth Nick spent his days tethered to that with a one-inch chain. We fed him there, so there were some bones and bits of meat and suet. Birds would zip in and scavenge. Jim said, "Look. See all those dead birds on the ground underneath that bush beyond his tether. How do you think they died?"

"Maybe the spoiled meat made them sick?" I suggested.

"No siree, lad. I happened to look out there a few minutes ago and saw him snatch a starling off one of those branches from at least ten feet away—chain and all. He crushed and dropped it."

"Oh, that's awfully quick," I admitted.

Three days later I was taking him his meat in the morning. We were in a hot spell and since we had no air conditioning I had left Nick outside for the night. He seemed appreciative of the roast I was carrying. I would typically just toss it to him and he would catch a 2 ½ pound hunk and basically chuck, chuck, chuck it down whole, never letting it hit the ground. After I had done this I noticed just inside his perimeter the body of a skunk. It had a piece about the size of a softball right out of its back and shoulders. The chunk was on the ground, uneaten. Remarkably, there was no smell at all. I presume the skunk had been sneaking in at night for scraps and Nick was waiting, glad of the chance to stop the pilfering. As Jim had said, it was over before the skunk saw it coming.

Early the next week I discovered that Mr. Eady, the butcher, had included in our box a large, nearly meatless femur bone of a steer. Nick scorned it, so I brought it into the warehouse, where our foreman Wally Rourke and I had been teaching Nick to leap over a broom handle as he ran down the long aisle. We had him up to five feet—nothing for him—but it was the closest thing to a dog-game we ever got him into. Wally noticed the big bone, hitherto untouched by Nick. He suggest we each take an end and see if he would take it from us. We held it close to his nose—then suddenly he seized it with a deep growl (the only one I ever heard)

34

and crushed the bone in two, leaving each of us with only the knob ends. We simultaneously dropped them on the floor.

Jim happened by just then.

"So it will be for one of you," he said, and walked away.

Over the weekend, at Jim's suggestion, I contacted a well-known dog racer, Ernie Brunet, from Gatineau, Quebec. Jim had worked with sled dogs himself up north, and he followed the best racers and their teams. Ernie, he informed me, had won the North American championship in 1961 in Laconia, New Hampshire, and was something of a legend in those circles. Well, as it happened, Ernie was glad to come and pick Nick up. He had a well-equipped dog truck and with a big piece of meat as encouragement got him into the largest cage.

With Nick as his lead "dog," Ernie won a lot of races, all over the continent. Jim reported on these races, so as to make me feel a bit better.

I wish the story had ended more happily. It didn't. Some months later Nick escaped (Ernie claimed a rival had opened the pen), killed a slew of barnyard fowl and ran off across the fields. The Quebec Provincial Police were alerted and Nick was shot with a rifle from the highway after being spotted by a patrol officer.

Jim said simply, "I'm sorry too, Davey. But be thankful. It was going to be him or you—and I hope you will see the mercy in it now." I did—and I have since. Nick left his mark on the community around Arnprior. For one thing, there never was another break-in at "The Luggage," not even ten years after Nick had left us. But Jim Wright left a bigger mark, and not just on me.

Jim and his wife raised their children admirably—Ian, whom I knew well, and two daughters, Joanne and Ruth. Each of them went on to honor their parents and each remained attached to the Chapel, with their own families all core members of that small worship community. That is more than may be said for a lot of folks, whatever their religious convictions. Long after Jim's death he continued to be spoken of often in our parts, invariably with fondness. At this distance I still think of him as one of those souls whose quiet presence persists in memory for very good reasons. I am grateful to have known him.

THE OLD STEVENSON PLACE

IF YOU DRIVE THE River Road between Arnprior and Renfrew, just past Castleford, you should see a dairy-corn silo and derelict brick house on the left, and on the right, along the river, a string of cottages. This was the old Stevenson place, one of the best farms along the river until old Mr. Stevenson and his wife passed away within a year of each other, as I seem to remember. The farm was willed to their three sons, Ross, Andrew, and Delbert (or Donald; I can't be sure, for I never did meet him). I had no idea about any of the sons, really, until one summer day in 1958 I was driving my 1950 Meteor, heading toward Portage and then on to Shawville, when I heard the engine sputter and realized I wasn't going to make it to the corner store gas station at Portage. I turned in their lane and stopped, hoping to buy a gallon of gas.

Even as I got out I could see that the porch was rotting on one side, with chickens hopping over missing boards, and that one downstairs window was boarded up. Nevertheless, there was a car parked farther up the driveway, so I ventured to approach the kitchen door and knock. No answer. I knocked again. Then a voice came from inside, saying, "It's stuck. Go to the front door."

I did, glad to see that the porch in front of it looked navigable. I knocked again. It creaked open to reveal a somewhat bedraggled man in his late fifties or sixties, wearing a plaid shirt and coveralls. He was smoking a cigarette, and his fingers were stained yellow with nicotine.

"What do you want?" he asked, in a flat, uninflected monotone.

I apologized for the intrusion, explained my situation, and asked if I could buy a gallon of gas.

"No," he said, "we don't have a tank on the farm anymore."

"Where might I get some?" I asked, hoping he'd point me to a neighbor.

"I don't know. But my younger brother is due back anytime now from Renfrew. He's gone for some grub and a few cases of beer. He usually has a siphon hose in the trunk of his car. If he has any gas left when he gets here, maybe he could fix you up."

This didn't seem very promising, but I agreed to sit down on a stump on the porch and wait. He brought out a wooden chair for himself, and as he did I could see behind him what looked like a tent in the parlor. It was then I noticed that a stove pipe protruded from a galvanized upper panel in one of the parlor windows, and then elbowed up. Clearly a chimney of some sort.

"So, where are you from, lad?" asked Ross, for this eventually was given as his name, "and what is your name?" I admitted the required information, and Ross said, "Ah yes, I have heard of you Jeffreys. It would be your father who has all those horses and cattle over past White Lake."

"Yes," I said.

"Mus be a helluva lot of work and expense," said Ross. "We got rid of our beasts years ago."

I realized then that not only were the fences in visible disrepair, but there was no sign of grazing either—just a lot of tall weeds as far as you could see. No tractor either.

"You folks not in dairy anymore?" I ventured.

"Ha! No, not for many years. We three were left the place by our parents, but we hated the work and right away sold off the quota.[1]

Silence. He scratched the scraggly, half-grown beard on his chin.

"I see," I said, wishing Delbert (if that was his name) would hurry up.

---

1. A license to supply milk to a set limit.

"The three of us are bachelors," Ross continued. Then with a chuckle, "No woman would want to live in this damn old place now anyway. Andrew had a fling with a widow-woman from across the river in Quebec some time back, but we couldn't agree on where to put her and he didn't want to go over there and live among them frogs. Besides, he'd have had to take some kind of job."

"So does Andrew live here too, then?" I was asking questions I shouldn't have, now just out of nervousness. I really wanted to see Delbert come back.

"O sure, lad. Andrew lives here. He's asleep inside. Sleeps most of the day."

"So did you go into beef? Or crops?" I asked.

"No sir. Once we used up the quota-money we sold the machinery, then after that a cottage lot each year along the river front. That pretty well kept us for nearly fifteen years. After that we sold the top-soil off these river bottom fields to landscapers. But that's pretty well done now too."

Suddenly there was a scritch of gravel at the top of the lane, and I looked up to see Delbert. But it was a dark green pick-up truck instead. It rolled up behind my old car and a big man got out.

"Well, Ross," he said, "what do I have to pay you next spring to dig young cedars from your back pasture?"

"We can talk about that," said Ross, "but before we do, I wonder if you can help this young lad here who is out of gas."

"I might, if he doesn't need too much," said the big man. "Will a half-gallon or so do you?" he asked.

"It should get me to the corner store at Portage," I replied. "How much?"

The big man didn't answer, but reached down to the floor in front of the passenger side of his truck cab and brought up a metal gallon can and funnel. Without further ado, he transferred its contents to my tank.

"How much do I owe you?" I asked again.

"Nothing, lad. Just you do something like it when you meet somebody who needs your help sometime."

And with that, I bid the big man and Ross both thanks and goodbye. My car mercifully started. I backed out of the lane and was soon in front of the single pump at the Ontario side of the Portage dam. As the gas was going into my tank, I said to the man who was pumping it, "I'm glad to be here. I was stranded back at the Stevenson farm. Do you know them?"

"Oh yes, lad. They are a local legend." He stopped at five dollars as I had asked and set the nozzle back on its bracket.

"It seems that things there are really run down," I said.

"To put it mildly. That house ought to be demolished. The roof went years ago and they didn't like the price to fix it. Did you see the tent in the parlor?"

I confessed I had.

"First one of the upstairs bedrooms sprang a leak, so whoever was in that room moved out. Then another and another, so they moved downstairs. Andrew, I think, slept on his father's napping cot in the kitchen. Then the kitchen started to leak, so they moved the stove to where Ross and the youngest brother were sleeping in the parlour. You see that pipe sticking out of the window?"

"Yes," I said. "I did. Weird."

"You see how the pipe goes through a piece of tin where the glass was?"

"Yes."

"Well, if you could see on the inside, it was part of the old farm sign, "Stevenson's Dairy Farm.""

"They used the farm sign?"

"Yep. Ross had to get my brother Jerry to cut it to shape and put the hole in it, for they didn't even have tinsnips. Then the parlour started to leak, so they put up that tent. God knows what they'll do next."

"It must have been a decent farm once," I said.

"Decent? That was the best farm for miles around. If old Johnny and Mrs. Stevenson could see it now."

As I drove over the dam, heading to the Hamilton Farm on the Zion Line to see my friend Laird, I was filled with both wonderment and dismay.

Later, I asked Laird's father if he had heard about the Stevenson Place. He had.

"An unforgiveable waste," was all he would say.

Laird put it more simply. "A dishonor."

Other people might have responded in other ways. My mother, on hearing my account, called it "a perfect picture of sloth." Yet Laird's response—"a dishonor"—so measured and succinct, has over the years seemed to me most apt.

LAIRD

I FIRST MET LAIRD Hamilton at the Brethren Chapel in Renfrew, where we attended a Friday night Bible Study and Fellowship for young people, hosted by Bill McRae. We were both sixteen. A measure of the rarity of such opportunities is that there was nothing like it for Protestant teenagers in Arnprior then, or in Shawville (closer to where Laird lived) either. We had both just obtained our driver's licenses and were glad to be able to drive twenty-five miles to a place where we met other teenagers who shared our interests. What Laird knew, that I didn't, was that Bill McRae, who would go on to become President of Ontario Bible College, was a gifted teacher.

What struck me about Laird straight off was his mature demeanor and thoughtful seriousness about the study of Scripture. He was already more biblically literate than I, and though taciturn and careful of his words, each study would be graced by one comment from Laird that was distinctively deep and well-considered. Bill McRae was quietly, yet transparently, impressed. So was I.

Laird's family was in the cattle business, so we had more than one common interest. Despite the distraction of the gaggle of girls that attended (there was only one other boy), we found quite a bit to talk about before and after the study. Laird invited me to drive over to Rolling Acres Polled Herefords on Sunday afternoon, just over an hour's drive from our place, where I met his father and mother. After going to see some of the cattle on pasture we had dinner together. It turned out that Laird's father Westburn dominated every conversation in which he was present. Temperamentally, Laird was much more like his mother, Gladys, slow to speak but clearly perceptive. After dinner we got away from the table and Westburn's probing questions and narratives (he was undeniably a gifted story teller in the Scottish country tradition), and in the parlor Laird put a couple of his vinyl recordings on the old gramophone. I was introduced thus to the Blackwood Brothers gospel quartet. After that Laird became quite a bit more talkative. He was already a big fan of Appalachian gospel quartets, and would be till the day he died. During the years of our friendship I got a pretty good education in such matters, courtesy of Laird's prodigious knowledge of this whole field, its prominent artists, history of the genre, and so forth. Though he was not himself a singer, all through the sixty years of our friendship, transitioning through tapes and finally to CDs, it was clear that Laird found joy in this music like almost nothing else. Long before cassette players became available in trucks, Laird had a player with 12-volt adapter in the family pickup and later even put one in the cab of their big tractor so he could listen while plowing.

When I went off to college, Laird didn't. Westburn said he was needed, and though Laird would very much have liked to follow his sister Anna to Millar Bible College in Swift Current, he accepted his father's edict, as invariably he did in other matters. He used what money he had to buy books—especially books of theology and biblical commentary, as well as quartet tapes. When I would see him in the summers he would ask about the biblical courses I was taking at Wheaton, and I would ask him about what he was reading that he would recommend. The summer following my first year at Wheaton I can remember him asking about my course in 1st and 2nd Chronicles with Walter C. Kaiser, Jr., who was to become one of my most important teachers. His contribution was to introduce me to a book on Romans by Donald Grey Barnhouse, a Reformed preacher renowned for solid biblical exposition, who pastored a church in Philadelphia.

"Have you listened to Barnhouse on the radio?" Laird asked. It had never occurred to me that this was possible. "Try it on any clear Sunday night," Laird said. "I can't get good reception here at the house, but if I drive the truck up the hill above the Caldwell Place (a farm they rented), I can almost always hear him. Eight o'clock. You should try it."

So the following week I did. There is a rocky ridge up behind our house and barns. I got the truck up there, started working my way across the AM bandwidth, and sure enough, Barnhouse came through on "WWVA, Wheeling, West Virginia." That was quite a station. Lots of gospel music, some of it good. Also crazy mail-order ads between programs. One of my favorites was for "two engagement rings and a tombstone," all for fifteen dollars, plus shipping. No kidding. But I became something of a fan of Barnhouse. Laird and I would periodically discuss the sermons. After a couple of summers of such conversation, often involving things I had learned in college and that he had learned from books, select radio listening, and audio tapes, it occurred to me that while I knew some things he didn't, Laird's general biblical knowledge and theological acumen were superior. Moreover, he was reading as many as four or five books a week, a pace I never matched. Yet he was neither showy nor defensive about his considerable learning, and always open to revising what he thought when encountering fuller information or a better argument. I have never known a better exemplar of what my philosopher friends call "the virtue of epistemic humility." Anywhere.

I was shocked to learn in the fall of 1979 that Laird had been stricken with a heart attack. He was barely thirty-nine years old. At the hospital in Ottawa physicians did some reparative work and sent him home with instructions to take it easy for a few weeks. I came over to see him, and found him his usual cheerful self. Westburn, though, was grumbling about having to do so much more himself and seemed irritated at Laird and dismissive of his condition. I began to notice that there was tension and that Westburn seemed unreasonable. I could tell that Laird's wife Mary was troubled too, but when I asked Laird about it, he said little except that he hoped things would work out. Typically of him, he was being "a faithful spirit [who] conceals a matter," but it was clear that the situation had gone past the point where most other sons would rebel. Sensing that Laird needed support, I came by more often in the spring.

Sometime in April I was getting into my car to drive back when Westburn came out of "the trailer," a single-wide in which he and Gladys now lived. He wanted to talk. They had agreed to buy a bull from Earl Vescovi in Montana and a roping horse from someone in Saskatchewan. Laird was to go out and pick them up.

"I think it might be good for Laird if he had company. Do you think you could get away? It'll be in May—so university should be out for the summer."

I agreed, and on a cold but sunny morning early in May we rolled out of their lane in the big black 454 Chevy pickup with plywood sides and a horse trailer behind. By the time we had crossed the dam at Portage and were turning up the Trans-Canada Highway above Renfrew, Laird seemed to relax.

"How about listening to some real good gospel quartets?"

"Sure," I replied. By the time we got to North Bay I had been introduced to several quartets of whom, to that point, I had never heard. Laird was loving every minute of it—the Oak Ridge Boys, The Imperials, The Blue Ridge Quartet, Jubilee Quartet, The Kingsmen. You name it, he had at least one tape in his big black box, and he knew all about their history too.

I said, "You seem really happy to be on the road, Laird."

"Well, I guess I am," he replied. Then after a minute's silence, "I guess you can tell it hasn't been always so easy with Dad."

"I've noticed. And marveled at the way you handle it," I said. "You're a better man than I am. I'd have likely blown my stack a long time ago."

"The doctor in Ottawa said that's likely what brought on the heart attack. When he found I never smoked or drank, he just said, 'So, what's bugging you?'"

This was his way of admitting that he wanted to talk. We did. Though he tried at every turn to offer excuses for Westburn, representing what he took to be his father's point of view as well as inherent disposition, I persisted quietly in ferreting out as best

I could just enough of what had been going on to make a few tentative suggestions. By the time we stopped in Thunder Bay for dinner and sleep at a motel, we had covered a lot of ground. We prayed about it together.

The next morning we had breakfast early and struck out for Kenora and the Manitoba border. We listened to just one song that morning, the Oak Ridge Boys' version:

> Let us have a little talk with Jesus
> Let us tell him all about our troubles
> He will hear our faintest cry
> And he will answer by and by. . . .

This song, my discomfort with some of its lyrics notwithstanding, led to a talk about prayer.

"By and by," said Laird, and turned off the tape player. "That can seem like a long time. Have you ever wondered about that?"

"Indeed I have," I replied. This led to my opening up about my failed marriage, explaining more about why I lived all week in a small bachelor apartment near the university, coming home only on the weekends to catch up on the farm work. Laird had put some pieces together already, and intuited more besides. I confessed that I was about at the end of my strength, and not just because of my own unsuccessful surgery. There was a lot to talk about, as well as pray about, and other than our cattlemen visits with Don Mitchell at Klondike Farms near Douglas and Dale Willms east of Swift Current, it took pretty well all our time till we rolled up in front of Don and Anna's place.

Anna was very happy to see her brother, and well aware of the tension with Westburn. It was good to see how close she and Laird were.

The following day we drove out about mid-morning, heading south on Route 4, then straight onto Montana #191 till #87, heading south to Roundup, right in the middle of the state. The Vescovis' ranch is just a few miles west of that, right along the Musselshell River. All the way down we returned to our conversation, each of us grateful for the other's attentive listening, observations, and mutual prayer. We got off the road and into their lane with daylight to spare.

Earl drove up in his truck just as we were getting out of our rig. He was a pretty boisterous, burly, and big-handed man, enthusiastically hospitable. He wanted to show us some pens with young bulls right away.

"We can see a few before dinner," he said. "Jump in here with me and we'll go have a look."

We did. Both of us were ready for the diversion, because it had been "deep water swimming," as I called it, for the best part of three days.

"Let's not call it that," Laird said. "Remember? I never learned how to swim."

The Vescovis had some of the best looking 'cattlemen's cattle' you could see anywhere, Herefords both polled and horned. The bulls were rugged and four-square, the heifers were feminine enough to prove out like their mothers, many of whom we would get to see the next day out on the range. That night over supper we asked Earl about their 119V bull, which both Laird and I had used by A-I on heifers, because his calves were lighter weight and round-shouldered, easily delivered.

"I almost forgot about that one," said Earl. "Sold him back east in Canada to somebody—I can't recall the name just now."

His oldest son Joe happened to stick his head into the kitchen door just then to leave off mail, and he provided the name.

"Anyway, we would never use a bull like that out here now," said Earl. "Nowhere near big enough for our market." As purebred breeders, Laird and I were well aware of the fashion for taller, longer, heavier bulls. That was why we were here.

"Tomorrow," said Earl, "we'll take you over to see Moose. He's the blankety-blank future we are looking at now." Earl had a limited range of adjectives; most were present-participles of a verb not used in polite conversation. Men in the cattle business tend to express themselves with short, vigorous Anglo-Saxon words, many of which are spelled with four letters. Earl was quite a bit more profane than the average, as well as voluble, so you are reading an expurgated version here. In one way that is a loss, because it takes some of the edge off the strong contrast between him and Laird that was forming in my mind.

When we drove next morning into the pasture where Moose was keeping about forty heifers company, we were astonished at his enormous size; he was the largest and longest bull of that age I have ever seen to this day. We also saw a lot of heifers, some in pens, others in pastures with bulls. I was as impressed with them as with Moose, though obviously for different reasons. I picked out a dozen and wrote Earl a check. He and Doug would deliver them about six weeks later.

After lunch Earl asked if we would like to see some of the cows on their twenty-thousand acre lease. We were keen, and climbed into Earl's truck, Laird in the middle. As we pulled out of the driveway I noticed that a second house on the property had one corner smashed out.

"That was my sister's house till she died," said Earl. "Then we had some f*ing renters who wouldn't pay their f*ing rent and wouldn't f*ing move out. F*ing police were no help, f*ing lawyer neither. It was February, so I just put the big iron back end of this rig through the walls. It was thirty below that night. They moved."

By this time we were bounding over rough, hilly open terrain, climbing, at a speed that had my head hitting the roof of the cab. Laird shot me a high-eyebrow look and grinned. We came to a big gulch and Earl yelled, "Over there we can get to where they'll be a lot quicker!" He just put the truck over the rim and started down at closer to ninety degrees than you might think. I put my hand on the door handle, ready to jump.

"Ha!" said Earl, as we clattered to the bottom. "I wondered how long it would take you to do that!" Laird laughed too, and then we were up the other side, a little less vertical, the engine roaring.

We saw a lot of cows that day and some beautiful country. As we were heading back by their irrigated alfalfa fields along the river I marveled at the scale of their operation. The eldest son, Joe, had become a veterinarian and ran a large-animal clinic just where we came out on the paved road. Soon we were back at the ranch house in time for a hearty meal of steak and spaghetti—not your usual combo but satisfying. After a short evening of conversation about cougars, cattle prices, and bloodlines, we slept well.

Like everywhere in cattle country, breakfast is on the table by 6:00 a.m. While we were eating, Doug poked his head in the door to get a big breakfast "to go" from his mother and then say goodbye. He had a bull they sold to South Africa already loaded, and he was headed for the docks in New York.

"You be careful, Doug," said his mother.

"Don't you worry 'bout me, Momma," replied Doug, pulling a large revolver out of his kit bag. "If any of them punks tries to bother me, they'll learn quick."

Then, with a wave to us all, he was headed east. Once we got Laird's bull loaded and the horse trailer re-attached, we were ready to go as well. We thanked Earl and his wife and headed out their lane past the well-ventilated rent house.

For the first couple of hours we reminisced on our visit with the Vescovis, then listened to some gospel quartet tapes. We made it to Swift Current in time for a late lunch at Laird's sister's home, then went on north on Route 4 past North Battleford to where Socks, the roping horse Westburn had bought over the telephone, was waiting to be picked up.

It was a pretty rough set up at the horse dealer's ranch. It was cold that afternoon when we loaded Socks and put in feed for her. The trailer was an open one, and we were worried about not having a horse blanket for her. One was found in a pile of old tack in a shed, and I put it on Socks. It turned out to be full of lice, some of which migrated from Socks to me. We fed and watered our passengers morning, noon, and night. The bull we never let out, whilst I would untie Socks and bring her to water so as to give her a bit of exercise. That's how I got lice in my jacket, I reckon. Poor Socks. I was taking quite a liking to her.

There was more talk about our respective troubles on the four day return journey. I learned that Mary was under a lot of stress too, loyal as she was to her husband. He learned, or confirmed, really, some different things. We did a lot of praying and recalled and discussed a lot of Scripture together. If we were friends before, we would be best friends ever after. I trusted in Laird's spiritual wisdom much more than I did my own; he was for sure the closest I ever had to what the Catholics call a spiritual director. Most of us recognize that it is possible to know someone quite well and not understand him. Apart from my beloved Kate, no one has ever understood me as well as Laird, and there has been no man whose counsel I would rather have or whose life of faithfulness I more often look up to.

If a person wanted to understand Laird Hamilton, all that would be necessary, in my opinion, is to read Psalm 15 and mull on it for a while. Simply put, Laird measured up; walking blamelessly, doing the right thing, speaking the truth in carefully chosen words, yet refraining from negative comment wherever possible, he honored the Lord in both deed and word. Once, when I had agreed on a price for a bull calf in the fall and the market shot up in the spring just before it came time to pick him up, I wanted to pay current value.

"No, Dave," he said. "I gave you my word and I'd like to keep it."

These qualities won respect for Laird far and wide, yet he did not ever have an easy life with his father. Westburn, despite some good qualities, continued to be a prejudicial and opinionated man to the degree that folks in the wider community shied away from his company. He had no obvious close male friends, whereas everybody liked Laird as well as respected him. In time it became clear that Westburn was jealous of Laird's friendships, especially as he would try to insert himself into each friendship in turn. Sterling McKibbon, another cattleman neighbor and long-term friend of Laird's, was one of these, and he and I worried together about the way Westburn seemed to undervalue Laird. While Laird himself was invariably quiescent about it all, and always principled about honoring his father, there came a time when it was obvious to everyone that Westburn was overtly favoring Laird's eldest boy Stephen over Laird to an unhealthy degree. Westburn took Stephen with him in the early fall of 1984 out west, visiting a number of ranches where we all had connections. including the Vescovis in

Montana. Laird stayed at home to do the work. By the time they returned Westburn was telling folks that he was going to will everything to Stephen, bypassing Laird. This occasioned a lot of stress, not only with Laird's mother and his wife, but with his sister Anna and husband Don. It wasn't that people didn't think very highly of Stephen; quite the contrary. Stephen was and is very much his father's son. What grated on everyone was Westburn's meanness and ingratitude with respect to Laird. Sterling and I were deeply concerned about this, and others like our mutual friends Laird Graham, Fred Shaver, and Barry Drummond worried too. The injustice of it was apparent to all.

Stephen, a superb young man and spiritually as well as temperamentally like Laird, was trapped between two orders of loyalty. His resolution to order his affections in such a way as to respect his grandfather but remain faithful to his father led to him turning down an opportunity to attend McDonald College for Agriculture near Montreal and go straight from being valedictorian at his high school graduation (and the recipient of six academic trophies) to taking up work on the farm—avoiding thus any written legal agreement pertaining to ownership. Privately, Stephen assured his father that any surprises occurring in Westburn's will would be quietly rectified.

Westburn gave up after the death of his wife Gladys. She was the spiritual center of the family, not only for Laird and Anna but for Mary and the grandchildren. Gladys was a woman of deep faith, gracious cheer, and, as she herself would confess, of a preference for mirth over any kind of distemper. Her loss was keenly felt, not least by Stephen and Laird. When in a few months Westburn took up with another woman, Pearl, the family were embarrassed and, to a visible degree, disheartened. Westburn moved to town in 1990 to take up residence with Pearl, which proved to be a blessing.

There was a need for pastoral presence in the Hamiltons' local congregation, Grace Community Church, and the elders asked Laird if he could take on a more regular role. He did, but always with an eye to welcoming a fulltime pastor. This was not to be.

Sunday after Sunday, week after week, Laird quietly went about the business of being the great pastoral presence I had always known him to be. Revered by so many within and without the congregation, and trusted by all who knew him, he yielded in the end to dropping the quest to fund and find a professional minister. They went on a typical Brethren Chapel model. Characteristically of Laird, however, he encouraged the church to affiliate with a supportive evangelical denomination, so as to provide for the future. The denomination chosen was the Associated Gospel Churches of Canada, which, it turned out, required an ordained minister. The elders debated. Then it occurred to some that they had never met an ordained minister who possessed anything like Laird's biblical knowledge, spiritual wisdom, or theological acumen. At his age, and with farm duties continuing, going to college and seminary would not be an option. Would the theologians from the seminary in Toronto be willing to give Laird consideration as an exception?

They were willing, depending on their own assessment of his theological formation. Three professors drove the six hours from Toronto and stayed for two days. The exam was a "viva," oral questions and detailed answers. The professors were astonished at Laird's knowledge, his understanding, and his deep wisdom. The qualities mentioned by St. Paul in Titus (1:5-9) had already been given ample witness by the elders. He was ordained.

Laird was universally recognized as the best pastor anyone in the church community ever had. People sought him out for counsel, even those who worshipped in different congregations, as well as people who went to no church at all.

After he was diagnosed with advanced bowel cancer, Laird continued to preach on Sundays. People have told us that, even on the Sunday two weeks before his death, you would have to know how gravely ill he was by other means: "he was just the same as always," one person told us.

I phoned him from Texas the following week, not only to check on him but specifically to express my deep gratitude to him for the influence he has had on my life.

"I have been blessed with some good teachers and pastors, Laird, but you have been more important to me than any. Before the Lord, I thank you. My debt to you is more than I can repay."

He was in great pain, but I knew he appreciated our conversation. A week later he was gone to his eternal reward, which I have little doubt is great.

"Lord, who shall dwell in thy tabernacle? Who shall dwell in thy holy hill?"

I still think about Laird Hamilton each time I read the fifteenth Psalm, and I have often mentioned my friend when teaching it, whether at home in the Ottawa Valley or here in Texas, more than two thousand miles away. Laird was "real" in a way very few people are. He made more than a few people think they should try harder to be real themselves. It doesn't take much effort to enjoy the colorful independent spirit of someone like Earl Vescovi, all the while appreciating his rough-diamond virtues. I thought well enough of him and his family that I let my oldest son, Bruce, spend the following summer working for him. But fully appreciating a quieter life of deep and settled virtue such as makes for a Laird Hamilton takes a lot more time. For several decades he was my closest friend, a treasure of grace for which I am eternally grateful.

FROM BEA TO ALICE

I THINK MOST UNDERGRADUATE students are generally respectful of their teachers; that was certainly the case at Wheaton College in the early 1960s. Given my comparatively unfashionable background and keen sense of how much I needed to do just to catch up to the general standards at Wheaton, that was especially true of me. I was not by 1963 academically speaking any longer on the endangered species list, but almost every class I took increased my astonishment at just how much there was to be learned. I began to want to learn as much as I could. Every course was intrinsically interesting to me.

I was greatly blessed in my teachers. Arthur Holmes, with his crisp English accent and exceedingly well-ordered mind, opened my own mind to philosophical thought. Gentle Joseph Spradley, in physics and especially in his wonderful honors seminar on the history and philosophy of science, fired a lifelong interest in his subjects. Walter C. Kaiser, Jr., who taught me Hebrew Old Testament and let me into a graduate seminar in biblical archaeology, inspired in me a love of the Hebrew Scriptures that has profoundly shaped my thinking and my spiritual character. Clyde S. Kilby, a most charitable man with a sparkle in his eyes, taught me to love the Oxford Christians (Lewis, Tolkien, Sayers, Barfield). All were excellent, and my debt to them is great. In some small way I have tried to live up to their example.

I had two other college teachers for each of whom my admiration is just as great, but whose character and challenge, ever prodding me even now, have nevertheless proved impossible to imitate. Each, for Wheaton College in that time, was counter-cultural; each was in her own very different way inspiring and endearing. Neither one could make sense of the other, or begin to enter into the other's alien culture. Both were single women, both brilliant, both a goad to the comfort zone of their male colleagues.

Beatrice Batson was the very epitome of a story-book Southern lady, always elegantly turned out in modest professional but feminine attire, of distinctly old Southern posture, speech, and manners (she had what earlier generations in Canada would have called "carriage"). In 1960s Illinois she was an anachronism, something out of the world of *Gone with the Wind*. She had earned her Ph.D. at Vanderbilt (George Peabody College) with Robert Penn Warren. These credentials did not in the least diminish her popularity with the students, especially women students, for whom she was a beacon, not least because she entirely outclassed the male professors in the English Department in energy, verve, and sheer force of intellect. A few men ventured into her classes, and not only English majors. Persuaded by many, and despite my mostly negative previous experience with female teachers, I signed up for her Shakespeare class.

What a revelation. We read sixteen plays in one semester; the pace was brisk. But her classes, typically Socratic in style, were the highlight of my week during the 1963/64 school year, coincidentally the year in which she won Wheaton's Senior Teacher Award.

"Alright, class. Now what do you think is going on in this monologue by Hamlet? What is its function in relationship to characterization? To Shakespeare's theme?"

Several pretty lame efforts at an answer would follow. Sometimes Dr. Bea would seem to groan, audibly.

"Now come on, class. Think!"

Eventually, either Steve Shoemaker or I would raise our hand from the back of the room.

"Alright Steve, what have you to offer us on this point?" Steve would offer.

"Now that is more like it. Class, can you see why Steve's answer helps us?"

Dr. Bea had no compunction about making her students feel uncomfortable—one of many character traits that would be out of fashion nowadays. In fact, for many students, as one of the young women who adored her told me, "She is terrifying!"

She also had no trouble making distinctions. Typically in her classes, I learned, there would be perhaps two or three whose focus and acumen were sufficient to please her now and then, and she made no attempt to disguise this. Many years later, Linda Petersen, by then chair of the English Department at Yale, said to me, "Dr. Bea is no democrat. That is essential to her genius as a classroom teacher. She is totally devoted to raising the intellectual caliber of her students, but doesn't get chummy or sentimental about their illusions." She went on to say that she owed her career choice to Beatrice Batson, but observed (this was in the late 1970s) that "somebody with her standards and *belle dame* classroom style would not be tolerated by my colleagues at Yale today."

For honors credit I also took an independent one-credit reading course with Dr. Bea, in which I read all the rest of the known Shakespeare canon, wrote a paper on the authorship of the disputed *King Henry VIII*, and took an exam. I also signed up for her seventeenth-century seminar the same term. It was a whirlwind. Poets dominated the seminar readings, especially Herbert and Donne. Her admiration for these poets was maximal, but in the case of Donne it seemed to all of us more like enchanted adoration.

"I think she is in love with John Donne," said one of my female fellow-students. She may have been at least partly right. Dr. Bea evidently took a visceral pleasure in the "Jack Donne" poems. One day she gave a reading of "To His Mistress, Going to Bed": "Off with that girdle," she laughed. "Now *that*, class, is a direct approach!"

"License my hands and let them rove," she recited, gustily, and laughed. "He may have been a divine," she chuckled, "but he was wonderfully earthy too."

Some of the women looked at each other. At least one in my line of vision blushed. After class Steve Shoemaker and I went to the Student Center for a coffee and a chat. "Well, she talks a lot about paradox. She *is* a paradox," I said. "An elegant, high-brow spinster lady gustily reciting a poem none of her male colleagues would touch with a barge-pole in class."

Just then, one of our female classmates was passing, and having overheard me, turned and said, "You might consider that her singleness owes to her never having met a man who could measure up to John Donne." She said this in a somewhat scornful way.

"Hmm," said Steve, "I guess they just don't make them like they used to."

Debbie cut off our laughter with a smart rejoinder: "That seems to be the case, gentlemen," and walked away. ("Gentlemen" was an overt Dr. Batson-ism.)

In retrospect, I can now see that in some fanciful way I had something like a crush on Dr. Bea. It occurred to me to think that if we lived in the Middle Ages she would have been just the sort of idealized though unapproachable woman that knights would willingly enter jousts for, risking death for the favor of her approving smile. That was silly, of course, but it did occur to me.

In the fall semester of 1964, however, when I was absorbed in classes in philosophy, physics, and Hebrew Bible and no longer her student, something like a modern poor analogue happened. Once again, it involved Steve Shoemaker. We were having coffee in the Student Union, having just come from a meeting of student writers. One of Steve's many women friends slid into our booth to share some disturbing information. Dr. Bea had confessed to two or three of her women students that she would probably have to consider leaving Wheaton. The reason was that her salary was not making it possible for her to manage the high and rising costs of living in that western suburban Chicago town. One of the students had asked her how her male colleagues, all but one married and with children, were managing. Dr. Bea's answer was that they were paid more precisely because of their roles as family providers.

We were stunned, unable to imagine that the best teacher in the English Department, and the one with the most prestigious doctoral pedigree, would be paid less than some of the men, not a few of whom were almost embarrassingly marginal.

"How much less?" I asked.

"She wouldn't tell us," was the answer.

After the bearer of this gloomy news departed, Steve and I began to consider what we could do. It occurred to me that one of our classmates in Dr. Bea's Shakespeare class, and one of her most ardent female supporters, worked in the Bursar's office. She seemed approachable, though I had never actually talked with her.

To make a long story short, it was arranged that I should indeed talk to her. Could we get from her a sense of Dr. Bea's salary in comparison with that of the men? She was willing to be helpful, and within a week we had discovered that Dr. Bea was paid only about two-thirds the salary of men with comparable years of teaching at Wheaton. We immediately composed an article (mostly me, I confess), which appeared on the front page of the next week's *Record*, the student newspaper. It began, "It has come to our attention that the acknowledged best teacher in the English Department is paid only a fraction of what her male colleagues earn." We gave numbers—not actual salaries, but percentages. Within an hour of the *Record* appearing, virtually all copies were gathered up from their locations on campus, and even removed from student mailboxes. Within a matter of hours, Steve and I were summoned by the President, severely chastened, and the *Record* was ordered to remove us as staff writers. As lead author, President Armerding informed me, he held me chiefly responsible. He demanded that I reveal the source of my information. I refused. This was—ahem—not appreciated.

I later learned that Dr. Bea was herself accused of complicity. She had, of course, no knowledge of what we were doing but was unjustly held in suspicion anyway. A couple of weeks later I saw her walking across campus toward the library; her path intersected with my own. She said simply, "I am forbidden to talk about this.

In fact, I am not sure that what you did was completely ethical. But thank you anyway."

We parted in the foyer of the library, leaving it at that. Years later we were both able to laugh about it. Best of all, she told me what I had (by other means) already learned—that the administration raised her salary in the academic year 1964–65, giving her parity with her male colleagues.

In those days, such issues of inequity were only beginning to come to light. Dr. Bea was not in our sense a feminist, and nobody has ever accused me of being one either. But it was a moment. Dr. Bea was the same age as my mother, and I am certainly no John Donne or a medieval knight, but her principled admonishment of my mischief, followed as it was by her affectionate gratitude, made me feel as though I had at least entered the precincts, if not the court, of her respect. We remained friends for the rest of her life, and her excellence, in so many respects, inspires me still.

The same fall semester that all this took place I was taking German and Russian from Alice Raven Naumoff. A more different person from Dr. Bea could scarcely be imagined. Miss Naumoff (she corrected me when I addressed her as "Dr. Naumoff," saying that she was still completing her dissertation) was plainspoken, as casually dressed as the Wheaton protocol would permit, and with her coke-bottle glasses, Brooklyn accent, and abrupt, exclamatory manner and funny asides, utterly unlike anyone else who taught at Wheaton. Her manner in class alternated between astonishing informality, razor-sharp philological insight, and overtly moral and intellectual admonition. She illustrated her points with bizarre Jewish jokes and Yiddish phrases. Born of illegal immigrant parents from Poland and Lithuania, she had been raised as an Orthodox Jew, but through the influence of Jewish Christians had become a Messianic Jew, the first I had ever encountered. Like no other teacher I have known, she used irony as a rod and staff, and many of her sheepish students did not find it all that comforting. All, however, found her funny; I, frankly, thought her hilarious as well as super-smart, and after the first couple of weeks of culture shock I looked forward to the high moments each class would bring.

I think it was most likely because of my being a relatively quick study where languages are concerned that Miss Naumoff took an interest in me. I got asked more than my share of questions. I noticed that she took pleasure in my efforts at accurate pronunciation, and so I increased my attention to getting it right.

"So, what's a big, overgrown guy from the Canadian wilderness doing at Wheaton?" She asked this one day as she sauntered into class, black satchel in hand. Grinning.

"It's an accident," I said. "My aunt Mabel overruled my parents."

"You should not say 'accident,'" she replied. "With God, nothing is an accident."

She seemed genuinely puzzled at mid-western culture generally and Wheaton culture especially. Often she would make indiscreet remarks about her sense of the weirdness of everybody but herself in class. She would also make random, disconnected comments on the environment. "So many big trees. Trees make me nervous. They could fall on a person. And so much green grass: is it really necessary? In Brooklyn people don't have to mow their concrete." Then she'd laugh.

"Why are Christians here so unjoyful?" she said once. "They take themselves too seriously. They should consider taking God more seriously—if they did that they would smile more. Maybe even laugh, God forbid." Again, peals of laughter.

"Too German, I think:" she was on the same track in another class one day. "Germans are only happy when everything fits into a tight system. *Alles ist ordnung.* And even then they are not entirely happy."

Alice Naumoff, though a teacher of German, had lost many family members in the Holocaust. Even so, her classroom comments would be considered over the top today, and her casual manner with students and colleagues certainly at the edge of unprofessional.

One day she saw me walking into the Student Union Building and called out loudly from quite a long way off, "Hey, *grotz nebische goy!*" I turned to see her sauntering (the only word I can think of that hints at her comical way of walking) in my direction.

"Got time for coffee?" I was surprised but made the time.

When we sat down she asked me, "So do you think that God is fed up with the Jews?"

Out of nowhere. I didn't know what to say. "What do you mean?" I asked.

"A lot of the teachers in the Bible Department seem to think that God has no place for the Jews because so many of them rejected Christ. They think Christians are the New Israel, and that God no longer cares about what happens to Jews."

I didn't know this. "Really?" I said.

"Really. I have talked to several of them. They are supercessionists." I hadn't heard that term before either, but she explained it.

"Something doesn't quite make sense to me," I said at length. "I can't see God going back on his promises to anyone—Abraham, Isaac, Jacob, Moses."

"Great! Now where do you get that idea, so different?"

I paused. "I guess just from reading the Bible."

"Good for you! You just keep on reading the Bible and ignore those Germanic systematic (she rolled her eyes and huffed the word) theologians. You know something about God that they don't."

All of this was quite bewildering to me at the time, but it set me to thinking about more than German and Russian.

The main thing about language classes is getting it right. Memory, and usage embedding memory, brings language to life. Alice Naumoff added another dimension by making me see that languages each have, in a sense, their own 'soul' or group personality. One day she said to me, "Okay—you—the tall Canadian: how do you say 'welcome' in French?"

"*Bienvenu,*" I replied.

"Quite true. Now say it is German."

"*Wilkommen.*"

"Exactly. If you want to show a bit more enthusiasm you have to say '*herzlich wilkommen*'; otherwise nobody thinks you really mean it. So now, Jeffrey, say it in Russian."

Well, the Russian of my beloved nineteenth-century novels, like the Russian she taught, was filled with passionate hyperbole, yet I couldn't remember the right answer.

"I'll tell you," she said. "It's *dobro pozhalovat.*"

This phrase has to do with the custom of welcoming or greeting someone with a kiss on each cheek. The literal meaning of the phrase is "I want to kiss you."

"So, do you sense a difference? German is a cool personality language. Russian is very warm by comparison. Effusive. It expresses a different group personality. Now, say it in Yiddish," she asked, with a twinkle in her laughing eyes. Of course, I couldn't. I can't remember her Yiddish, but I do remember her translation: "Come on in already! Nice to see that you aren't dead yet!"

Sometimes you forget that idioms come and go, that what might have been, say, appropriate in the time of Chekov or Lermentov, could ossify or even vanish. I learned this the hard way fifty years later when friends brought along a colleague and his wife visiting from Belarus to dinner. I greeted them at the door in my remembered Russian.

"*Dobro pozhalovat!*" I said, looking at Alexi's wife, who I was meeting for the first time. She half lurched in my direction, surprising and embarrassing me mightily. Alexi is a very literal man, as are now most post-WWII Russians. He growled, "Why do you want to kiss my wife?"

Oops. Thank you, Alice Naumoff. But I have never forgotten her basic lesson. To every language there belongs not only a distinct grammar and lexicon, but a particular consciousness, best expressed in that language.

Alice would once in a while illustrate this point further by rhapsodic comments about a Polish poet on whose work she was writing for her NYU dissertation, the title of which was "Ivan Konevskoj: Mystical Symbolist Poet of Nature." He seems to have been a rather obscure figure, but she clearly thought well enough of his work to keep at it; she did not finish and receive her Ph.D. until 1969, five years after I was her student.

Dr. Bea had a long and illustrious career at Wheaton before her retirement, founding and directing a center for Shakespeare studies. She was active as a scholar long after she retired from the classroom, and remained intellectually sharp and of excellent memory almost until her death in 2019.

Alice Naumoff, despite her good Ph.D. in Slavic Studies, taught intermittently in a few liberal arts colleges, but eventually moved to Germany, where she entered a community of Protestant Christian women. I cannot find that she ever published anything as a scholar. Then, in 2018, she took up permanent residence in Nariya, Israel, very near the Lebanese border, which is where I at last caught up with her by mail, thanks to my wife Katherine's sleuthing. She is very active in leading Bible studies "all over Israel," as she put it, in Hebrew, Russian, and German as the situation requires. Once I had written her, she replied in characteristic form. "Hey, you should put those languages of yours to work. Get on over here and help us!"

Heh. Two remarkable women, so different from each other, but both great teachers and real characters. I am eternally indebted to each of them. It has since occurred to me more than once that despite mathematics having always been my strong suit, I wound up doing my own Ph.D. in English and Comparative Literature. Alice would say, "*a moshel iz nit kain reï'eh*" (an example is no proof), but in my life it seems to have worked when no proof was available.

D.W. ROBERTSON, JR.

I FIRST ENCOUNTERED PROFESSOR Robertson during the beginning week of my graduate work at Princeton. Unfamiliar as I was with Firestone Library, I was wandering in the B floor, endeavoring to be sure I had found the seminar room assigned to my Chaucer course before the scheduled 2 p.m. starting time. I passed an odd-looking man perusing books in the open stacks. He was wearing a somewhat tattered grey sharkskin suit jacket, but with khaki trousers that didn't match, a white tee-shirt only under the jacket, and cotton tennis shoes. I took him to be a janitor, perhaps, and asked for directions. He arched his bushy eyebrow, gave me a well-creased Uncle Screwtape smile, and pointed the way.

"I'll be there in a minute," he chortled. Sure enough, just after I took my seat at the table with eight or nine other graduate students, the "janitor" strode into the room.

"Harff!" (His laugh was like the bark of a large dog.) "I gather that some of you think you want to learn a little about Chaucer." Here he arched his eyebrow again, his eyes glittering as he surveyed the room, much as might a fox at his leisure in a pen of chickens. "Harff! Well then, let's begin, shall we?"

The effect of his unprecedented weirdness, not just his anomalous appearance (remember: this was Princeton, in the preppy, Little Lord Fauntleroy days of the mid-1960s), was deeply unsettling. Most of us, I one of them, were looking down nervously at our note-pads, pens in hand.

"Robbie," as later we learned to refer to him amongst ourselves, began as follows.

"Chaucer lived and wrote under the reign of three kings. Edward III, who established the chivalric Order of the Garter, was a good king. After his death, things deteriorated significantly. John of Gaunt, regent protector of Richard II, was strong but erratic. Richard was weak—a political disaster. Chaucer was close to the court; his patron was John of Gaunt. He was influenced profoundly by the political decline and loss of English prestige during much of his life."

Robbie continued on to sketch out the relevant political history, the impact of the Black Death and Peasant Revolt.

"So how much does Chaucer tell us about his experience of the Plague?" Silence. "Not a damn thing," he snorted. "In which of his poems does he tell you about his personal feelings?" Again, silence. "In none of them," Robbie snorted. "His audience would not have been interested in his personal feelings. They had not, like you, been seduced by romanticism and—harff—existentialism. Chaucer was not sentimental. He might well have liked Mozart, because his music is rational and mathematical, but would have despised Tchaikovsky and all the schmaltz written after that. He was a serious Catholic. In his view faith was rational, and sin was irrational. Moreover, all sin was social—damaging to others. For Chaucer, sin was an enemy of love; for us now it is more likely to be a name for perfume. There was yet no valid conception of secret sin. Emotions and feelings had nothing to do with it." He raised the already famous right eyebrow and scowled at us. "To read Chaucer credibly you are going to have to get your facts straight, work rationally from the context afforded by texts he read and not any 'hearts and flowers' modern critic; and you are going to have to learn Middle English, some French, and Latin well enough that you won't be making idiotic mistakes about what he has written."

Another pause to scowl as if in a sweeping condemnation of all any of us had been taught.

"And you are going to learn literary conventions from classical to Renaissance literature, and *un-learn* the subjective and unwarranted hogwash you have doubtless been accustomed to."

Robbie went on like this for three hours. Our heads were spinning. We felt like rubes.

The second class was much the same in tone, though Robbie had launched into a line-by-line exposition of the General Prologue of *The Canterbury Tales*, verbally footnoting everything with rhetorical, literary, and philosophical as well as historical vectors.

"Now consider the Wyf of Bath. How many husbands had she?"

"Five," somebody said, "and the one she is now with she isn't married to."

"Harff!" replied Robbie. "So who should that remind you of?"

Silence. Then I said, cautiously, "The woman by the well in John 4?"

"Well now," chuckled our professor, "and how should we imagine Chaucer to have understood the figural meaning of that story?" I hadn't a clue, and most of the others were similarly blank. Then one fellow, a returned Rhodes scholar from Oxford, said, "As an allegory, I presume."

"An allegory of what?" demanded Robbie. When he received no answer, he began to recite, from memory, moral, allegorical exegesis of John 4 from Augustine through to obscure biblical commentators of the eleventh through thirteenth centuries.

"And you can find all of these and more in the *Patrologia Latina*," he said gruffly. "I expect you to make use of it."

"Er, sir, but is there an English translation?" asked a sweet-tempered but very nervous fellow-student named Sam Josloff.

"Harff!" was the reply, "and why would you be needing a translation? You all have to pass the Latin exam. I assume you know that. This will be good practice for you."

He continued.

"Now as St. Bruno Astensis would tell you, to be '*som-del deef*' is to be obtuse to the precepts of Scripture. How reliable a reader would you expect the Wyf to be?"

"Presumably not very," said the Rhodes scholar.

"Another thing," said Robbie, "just because some words in Chaucer's text are familiar to you, you should not assume you know what they meant in the fourteenth century. Take the Knight, who is defined in the General Prologue by what he loves: *"trouthe, honour, freedom, and curteseye."* None of those words now retains its primary medieval meaning. Take a look in the full OED and see what the words meant then, and make that a practice. Our primary concern at this level is to do our best to understand what Chaucer and his first audience thought he meant to say. The last thing we need is some version or other of "this is what it means to me. Harff!"

Robbie's method was exegetical and historical as well as philological, and he was always confounding us with sources that seemed to me unnecessarily esoteric (I began to lump the most obscure of these together under the nomen St. Broadbottom of Bumblethorpe), and on this occasion such a source was given as explanatory for the Wyf's claim,

> For wel ye knowe, a lord in his household
> He nath nat every vessel al of gold,
> Some been of tree, and doon hir lord servyse.

"The vessel of wood," says St. [Broadbottom of Bumblethorpe] signifies a vessel 'unto dishonor,' like a chamber-pot."

"But why do we need the commentator?" I finally asked, "when she is simply quoting verbatim St. Paul in 2 Timothy 2:20?"

This happened a few more times. Finally one day Robbie looked at me and huffed, "Well, since few but you seem to know the biblical texts, why don't you make it your business to make us a dictionary of such matters?"

He seemed aggressive and dismissive at the same time, but later he remarked, also in seminar, "We are soon going to need a prerequisite course in the Bible for all seminars up to the Enlightenment." I began to think he was more than half-serious.

Stories about Robbie, mostly by way of former doctoral students but occasionally via other faculty members, *sotto voce* in the library, helped me contextualize the man. Some of these stories now seem to have been of the urban legend type, but some have empirical support. He may well have been a child prodigy, rebellious, and bored beyond limit by public school—that has been the experience of many. Sunday School and church were evidently anathema to him, the preachers and teachers scorned as "sentimental fools" long before he graduated. He was extremely uncomfortable in social settings and downright awkward in personal conversation. I suspect that today he would be recognized as on the Aspergers spectrum and perhaps treated clinically. He was sent to the University of North Carolina at Chapel Hill, where he met challenging interlocutors, one of whom was the legendary Urban Tigner Holmes. After three degrees there he went on to an instructor's post at Yale. Another of Holmes's former students, visiting Princeton, told some of the faculty that Robbie spent his undergraduate summers traveling with a circus as a magician and hypnotist. Apparently it brought in quite a bit of money.

His capacity for learning languages was staggering. The story that every time he learned a new language (which he did for amusement) he would write an article for a professional journal of history or literature in that language is probably apocryphal, yet somebody once showed me an issue of a journal in Lithuanian in which Robbie had published the previous year. We heard from two faculty members how a student from Columbia had been referred to Robbie for possible help with a dialect of sub-language related to Ge'-ez from a monastery on the upper Nile. The graduate student had transcribed the text in question (the language, though linguistically unrelated to Greek, was written in Greek letters). He brought his transcript down on the train from New York and went looking for Prof. Robertson in the faculty lounge. He was met at the door, and nervously reported that he couldn't find said professor in his office, though there had been an agreement with his own professor that he could have an appointment at this time. Robbie overheard.

"Oh, hell, I forget," he roared. "Why don't you just come in and tell me what you are looking for?"

The faculty lounge, of course, was strictly off limits to our own graduate students, a point mentioned by Tom Roche, the young Spenserian who recounted this event to a few of us.

The student came in and presented his transcription to Robbie. "What language is this supposed to be?"

The student reiterated (I don't remember the name).

"What? I don't know that one. Sorry."

He handed the transcription back without so much as looking at it, and the student, ashamed, confused, and dejected, rose to leave.

Just as he got to the door, Tom Roche recounted, Robbie roared at him: "Well, since you have come all this way, bring it over and let me have a look." Which he did and in less than two minutes Robbie said, "Harff! By God, I *can* read this. Take that pad and pen, and write this down."

The voice reading, line by line, took only a few minutes, apparently—the passage was not lengthy. Astonished, grateful to the point of tears, the student gathered up his treasure and stumbled out.

Stories like this were one thing; watching Robbie in the reading room was another. Once I observed him with several volumes of the *Patrologia Latina*, reading, then opening another volume, reading, until finally after about an hour, he closed all the volumes, took out three 5"x8" cards and began writing. Another student deliberately passed behind him so he could look over his shoulder to see what it was. After Robbie had re-shelved the volumes and left, we all gathered to hear.

"Quotation mark. Then long passages in Latin. Then quotation mark. Then what looked like "Silvestris" and the PL volume and column number!"

Plainly put, the man was terrifying. And not just to his students.

Picture, if you will, our seminar on the opening day of Robertson's course in Old Irish. There were eight of us, representing specialties in medieval English, Old High German, Medieval French, Spanish, Old Norse, and Sanskrit. Robbie strode into class muttering to himself.

"Harff!" He looked around the table. "You sure you want to do this? Harff!"

Most of us just shrugged our shoulders.

"Well, I haven't taught Old Irish now for fifteen years, and as I was walking in this morning it occurred to me that a reasonable way to begin with this group is to show how Old Irish is an Indo-European language. Despite some distinctive features, it has deep relationships with most of them. For example: Jeffrey, give me a common noun in Anglo-Saxon."

"*Hlaf-weard*," I said.

"That's a compound. Pick one or the other."

"Okay, *hlaf*."

"Good. You—what's your name?"

"Nelson."

"Give me a strong verb in Old Norse."

He did, and so on around the table, from weak verbs through participles and the like. Then, to the fellow from Sanskrit, "Give me the most common copula."

All this time he had been making columns across the blackboard for our languages, whilst making a vertical row for each of our nominated lexical terms. After the Sanskrit copula there was accordingly a graph with one part of speech for each horizontal column. He had left a blank column at the far right, labeled OI. He then proceeded to fill in all the blanks, providing cognate terms for each language and then, at the last, Old Irish. This was the substance of the session.

To wrap up, he said, "Now Old Irish not only has declensions in the form of prefixes and suffixes, but it has in-fixes as well. With sound changes over time, some of the in-fixes change as well as do the initial sounds of prefixes. That's why there isn't a dictionary of Old Irish. Harff! Damndest thing. But you'll get used to it. See you next week."

I need hardly point out that rehearsing a polyglot demonstration such as we had just experienced is impossible. As we walked away, several headed for the men's room.

"Almost scared the shit right out of me there in class," said the Romance-language guy. "God help us. We're doomed."

Those who weren't in the men's room were standing outside, mostly staring at the floor.

"I think we need to visit the Annex," somebody said at last, to instant agreement.

All but the Sanskrit guy traipsed across Nassau Street and downstairs into said pub. Most ordered hard spirits; I, who had at that time no experience with such beverages, asked for a Michelob. We drank mostly in a silence broken now and then with a profane exclamation.

"We're doomed," was beginning to be a refrain. Some guys were repeat-ordering doubles. After two beers, I left.

The next week, to our mutual surprise, all but the Sanskrit doctoral student showed up. The course was mind-altering, painfully exacting, but in the end well worth it.

I owe Robbie a great deal. Though I might have felt squelched by him, he somehow brought out what was needful. He thought C.S. Lewis's book, *The Allegory of Love*, was one of the most ignorant books ever written, on a par, he said, with "the fantasies of Gaston Paris." Well, it turned out that he was more right than not in this judgment (he admired greatly, however, *The Discarded Image*). I have often since reflected that while Robertson was as averse to Christian apologetics as Lewis was good at it, his superior knowledge of medieval theologians and philosophers was precisely what I needed to learn at that stage of my life. Robbie derided the early Franciscans because they reminded him too much of the simplistic pieties he had rejected as a boy. He thought John Wyclif an intemperate and puritanical belligerent such as his sane and realist Chaucer could never have admired. When I announced my desire to do my dissertation on Franciscan spirituality and vernacular poetry, then later to look into Wyclif's influence on so many of Chaucer's court friends (they both had John of Gaunt as patron), Robbie fairly bellowed at me, "Good God, Jeffrey! Are you just completely bone-headed?"

One day we met to discuss my research plans. "Do you know Provençal?" he asked.

"Er—no."

"Well, if you are going to read these troubadours you'll need it. It should take you about three weeks, since you have French and Latin. Come back and see me then—with the edition of the Provençal poets in hand."

It was an awful three weeks, but I did work at it. When the time came, he had me sit across from him and translate off the page verbally.

"No! Good God, where did you get that reading from?" and then he would proceed to decline the verb as it ought to have been; this was repeated a number of times. I was mortified. "Well, I suppose you could have done worse," he concluded, "but not much."

He made me learn some Italian and demonstrate by sight-translating texts in the same way.

But in the end he directed the thesis (with considerable help from his former student and junior colleague John Fleming, who, it turned out, was knowledgeable and sympathetic to my proposal).

Robbie had some social scruples which surprised me. Almost all of our professors smoked in class: E.D.H. (Dudley) Johnson, for example, would begin class by setting out before him on the seminar table a pipe, two cigars and a pack of cigarettes, and by the end of class they were usually all used up (when he was either pleased or distinctly displeased he would emit great clouds of smoke); Marjorie Hope Nicholson would set out three packs of unfiltered Camels and nearly finish them, lighting each new cigarette off the butt of its predecessor, and only every few minutes exhaling a little wisp of smoke out of her left nostril. Robbie, by contrast, though he smoked cigarettes, never afflicted us by smoking in class. Another scruple was revealed the year after my seminar with him; he heard that for the first time in his career there would be a female graduate student in his class, and so he showed up in a neat suit, polished shoes, and wearing his Robertson family tartan tie, which seems to have been the only tie he owned.

As I was leaving for my first job, Robbie asked to see me. He apologized for having to be told when I was due to take the general exams (he couldn't place me), and in advance for not being likely to be in touch very often by mail. "I am not a very sanguine person," he said simply. I understood, surprised even that he should feel it necessary to say so.

Several years later, on the occasion of Robbie's retirement (1980), I was one of the half-dozen people invited to speak at a symposium in his honor. My paper was on the pertinence to Chaucer's *House of Fame* of the hermeneutics of John Wyclif. In the Q&A, the great man rose to register his dissent. He had quite a bit to say. I was staying with John Fleming and his wife, and at a reception the following evening I said to John, "Well, I see that I have yet to satisfy our mutual mentor."

"David," he replied, "yours was the only paper in the entire colloquium he responded to at all—that was a signal honor."

"Honor?" I laughed.

"You are the youngest person on the program," said John. "He respects you because you aren't an acolyte. If I were you, I'd take his going after you as one of the best compliments you have ever had. Period."

I accepted his rebuke. Robbie was the farthest thing from a disciple-maker. I wish there were more like him.

SISTER GIOTTO'S FLORENCE

I FIRST WENT TO Firenze in January 1968. Florence was hard to get to by plane; my flight from London took me only as far as Milano, from whence I made my way by train through valleys and cone-shaped hills, with angled vineyards and candle-shaped Cyprus trees that looked as though Giotto had painted them. I had thought those features in Renaissance painting a defect of emerging realism; suddenly, they were a backdrop to penumbral realities of postwar Florentine culture into which I was headed, having little but letters of introduction to librarians and a few addresses in my possession, including the Pensione Adria, on the bank of the Arno abutting the south end of the Ponte Santa Trinita. And a crude street map of the city.

It was warm enough that my decision to walk from the train station, suitcase in one hand, briefcase in the other, was less than wise. By the time I made my way past Santa Maria Novella to the Arno, then up to Santa Trinita and across—less than a mile—I was soaked with perspiration. When I was shown to my room I immediately poured myself one glass of water after another. Only later did I remember the warning given me by some friends before I left: "Remember; they are not yet done cleaning up from the flood. Whatever you do, don't drink the water!" An hour later I walked into the top of Piazza del Carmine and found, as the *portieri* told me I would, a nice little ristorante. I ordered the dish he recommended, *insalata el polo.* While I was waiting, I noticed people at the next table pouring red wine over their salad. What an odd thing to do, I thought.

Well, not so odd it seems. Later, when I had become so ill that my eyes were yellow and I couldn't work further than a few steps from whatever *cabinetto per uomini*, I went to a doctor. He prescribed medicine to combat my Hepatitis A, but it was three weeks before I returned to anything even faintly resembling normal. Whether from the tap water or the salad, I had discovered why my more experienced friends back at Princeton had warned me about the water. The 1967 flood had ruptured sewage lines and contaminated the Florentine water supply. As to Hep Λ, if I may borrow a phrase from Shakespeare's *Hamlet*: "It out-Herods Herod. Pray you avoid it."

It was thus that I began my manuscript research at the Biblioteca Nazionale pretty much collywobbled. Also, I began to follow scrupulously the advice of my rather sour-puss doctor, "*Niente piu acqua! Bere vino!*" making exceptions only for coffee and the odd small bottle of Coke. Once I realized that a full regular bottle of Antinori red cost the same as the Coca-Cola, on sound Scots principles I stopped drinking Coca-Cola. The meds helped some with my *stomaco malato*, though I had some pretty explosive episodes, and my eyes were yellow for weeks.

My second evening in Florence I had an invitation of some weeks' standing to dinner at the apartment of Carolyn Valone, introduced to me via mail by Prof. Thomas Roche, the Spenserian at Princeton, who referred to his friend as "Lady Carolyn." She lived at 13 Via Ginori in the Borgo San Larenzo neighborhood. The *portieri* there showed me to the ancient *ascensiore*, an open cage with visible chains like those on a bicycle. Eventually it got me to the *terzo piano*. I knocked at the door, which was opened to reveal Carolyn herself, a short, plumpish, and vivacious post-doctoral student. She said, "Welcome to Florence!" and then ushered me in to where another woman, dressed like a religious, was standing by the table.

"This is Sister Giotto!" said Carolyn. "I wanted you to meet her right away. She is the perfect guide to this wonderful city!"

"*Buona serra*," she smiled, "you are just in time for some terrific antipasto that I picked up on the way over here."

"*Mille grazie*," I said in my fledgling Italian.

"Oh, skip the Italian. At least for tonight. Carolyn and I are both Americans anyway. We'll get you speaking Italian soon enough. Red wine?"

"Okay," I said rather sheepishly. These Americanos were a bit on the boisterous side for me. Carolyn, with her dark hair and eyes, was of Italian descent, but not Sister Giotto. Her red hair, many freckles, and blue eyes marked her as more likely Irish. I was going to ask about her family name, then remembered: that's not what you do when you meet a nun.

"And just call me Giotto when it's informal like this. Skip the Sister stuff. We hear you aren't a Catholic anyway." She laughed.

"Giotto somehow managed to convince the whole Dominican Order back in the States that the feminine derivative of Ambrose was "Ambrogiotto," which she asked to be abbreviated then to "Giotto." She is a medievalist art historian too, and her favorite painter is. . ." (here Carolyn made a sweep of her hand toward her friend), "Giotto. Of course!"

Over dinner I got many recommendations of who and what to see when I wasn't in the library. Also an invitation to dinner the following evening at the home of Sergio Mariotti and his wife. They assured me that arrangements had been made and I was expected. Suddenly Giotto said, "Poor boy—I see you've been drinking the water!" This led to more awkward questions, followed by questions about our research and the discovery that we were all interested in the thirteenth-century Franciscan style change.

"Giotto doesn't get as much time for her research as she'd like," said Carolyn, "because of her work at the Gonzaga Art Institute."

"But it keeps me posted here," chirped Giotto. "Goodness knows—they could send me to Buffalo!"

"Armpit of the nation," observed Lady Carolyn. I could see by their lingo that these two characters were not at all given to courtly graces. They drank heartily, however, prompting me to an early exit, excused by my *probleme di stomaco*, as I learned, more delicately, to speak of it.

The following day Giotto and Carolyn were both waiting in Giotto's Cinquecento in the piazza below the Adria when I emerged at 8:30 p.m. Dinner at 9 p.m. was normal in Firenze then, but at Mariottas one had aperitifs at 9, with dinner itself on the table between 10 and 11 p.m. Now for the likes of me, even at 26 years of age, getting into the back of a rickety 1950s Fiat Cinquecento was no easy thing. It was not the convertible model, unfortunately. The car was tiny, tinny, and the back seat looked like it might do for a Chihuahua.

"We got Tom Roche in there okay," said Giotto cheerfully.

"But he's about 5'8" and not more than 130 pounds," I replied, grunting and huffing. Carolyn got out to facilitate my entry on all fours, but it felt like I needed a shoehorn to get in and might need a can opener to get out. To get a better appreciation of this, I recommend looking at an online picture of this breadbox with wheels. Small as it was, however, Giotto couldn't find a big enough parking space anywhere within three blocks of our destination. When she did see one hopelessly cramped spot, she said, "What if I just drive in and put my front wheels up on the sidewalk?"

"At the least you'd get a big *biglietto del parcheggio*," said Carolyn. "Or worse. They might just let the air out of your tires."

"Let me out of this thing," I offered, "so I can have a look."

I got Giotto to get the rear of the Cinquecento in as close as she could and asked her and Carolyn to get out. In that car the engine is in the back, and while it's not much bigger than an old Singer sewing machine, I figured I couldn't lift it from that end. But the front was just an empty trunk, so with a couple of heaves on the bumper I got it into the space with only about a foot to spare.

We were met at the door of the Mariottis' top-floor residence, not by Signora Mariotti but by Libby Batazzi.

"Libby! Meet our new Canadian friend, Paul Bunyan!" exclaimed Giotto. "David, this is the estimable genius who actually runs the Americano Book Store, though don't let her husband know I said so. Appearances are important!"

Introductions accomplished, we were ushered into the posh Mariotti apartment, with its view over the Arno and night-lit city. There were, in addition to Sergio's wife Marta, several other guests—Francesco, Libby's husband; Judy Chidester, a staff member at the American consulate nearby; and a scowling little man named Henry, who was a sales representative for some American company, along with his "escort," an attractive companion whose name was Gabriella. She seemed pleasant, and as I was put next to her in the parlor, I asked about her line of work (big mistake). She was a bit evasive but said that she worked as a "companion translator" for businessmen from North America and the UK. Just then Henry snapped, "She's with me. Get that?" Oh boy.

Sergio himself arrived late, as also did Francesco Batazzi—too late to overhear the discomfiting conversation about mistresses, prompted by Marta's unhelpful suggestion that Sergio was probably with his alternate *signora*. This led to an astonishingly frank conversation among the women about the practice, without a trace of rancor, but rather a complete sense of *che sera, sera*. I was nonplussed, embarrassed, and silent. Libby Battazzi's words in particular left me feeling like a stranger in a strange land for sure.

"I don't care except for two things—I don't want to know anything about it, and that she is clean."

"Clean is better than dirty," said Sister Giotto cheerily, and everybody but me, and Gabriella, laughed.

Getting to know Sergio Mariotti was my passport into the world of the men I came to think of as "the last of the Florentine princes." All were well off, all were very worldly, and they found time for soccer, for hunting boar on their villas, for fine dining, and, as I had just learned, for their mistresses. I was grateful that none of these ever introduced me to a mistress, and most never introduced me to their wives (though all of them seemed to be married).

The after-dinner drinks and conversation ended at 2 a.m., and after I squeezed once more into the back of Sister Giotto's wee car (the cars hemming us in had left), I asked whether any of the dinner guests beside themselves were Catholic.

"Oh, everybody," responded Carolyn. "There are hardly any Protestants around here."

"Francesco gave me a note for his brother Ferdinando, Fra Fernando, at Convento Ognisanti. I hope to meet him there tomorrow. But Francesco has a mistress?"

"Ha!" interjected Giotto. "Here everybody is a Catholic, and every married man keeps a mistress. That's an exaggeration, but not by much."

Giotto's car was chugging to a stop near my *pensione*, right by the end of the Ponte Santa Trinita.

"I don't get it," I said as I was getting out, awkwardly.

"Then you just don't get Italian Catholics!" said Giotto cheerily, "but you will! *Bienvenuto a Firenze!*"

As I began to walk to the door I noticed a poster attached to the end of the bridge. It read: "*I Fiorentini sanno daverro come vendere le mele*." "Florentines really know how to sell the apples?" I translated to myself. "What in the world does *that* mean?" Beyond doubt, I had entered a different culture.

Like the Psalmist I consider myself an ally of all those who honor God's law and seek to obey his commandments (Ps. 119:63). I had hoped to find the spiritual Franciscans of convent Ognisanti to be an amiable fraternity, and I was not disappointed. The brothers were active in the community of the poor, in care for widows and others in need. Six hours a day were permitted in the library/ scriptorium but were balanced by as many hours doing everything from fixing a widow's broken stair to hospital visits and acting as chaplains to the volunteer ambulance guild, a venerable Florentine descendant of the medieval confraternities that the Franciscans did much to organize and encourage. Fra Batazzi proved, despite his worldly brother and sister-in-law, to be a man of evident piety and enthusiastic spiritual affections. One evening we were discussing the relationship of poetry and prayer, a topic of major interest to me and, as it turned out, also to him. He didn't find English a very poetic language. In fact, he went so far as to say that it must be offensive to the ears of God (!), not so harsh and guttural as German, he allowed, but almost as bad.

"So I imagine you think Italian is better," I said with a smile.

"*Ha ragione, Signor Grande*," he replied. "Listen," he went on, "to this prayer I say every night before going to sleep." And he recited the first eighteen verses of John chapter one. "*Nel principio era la parola, e la parola e con Dio, e Dio e la parola. . ..*"

"Italian is more melismatic for sure," I admitted.

"Now listen to the prayer in Latin," he replied, and began, "*In principium erat verbum. . . .*" And when he had finished, he said something like, "I rest my case."

"I have two things to say in response. The first is a question: why do you call the prologue to John's gospel a prayer?"

"We pray these words at the end of every Mass here in Convento Ognisanti," he said simply. I did not yet know about *lectio divina*, nor even that in the Middle Ages, the period I was studying as to its spirituality in particular, this was a normative practice. He explained this to me.

"I think it may be that medieval English might seem more pleasant to the ears of God—and of his Italian Franciscan servant Fernando—than modern English."

"*Per favore recita*," Fra Fernando replied.

I began with the Lord's Prayer: "*Oure faeder, thu the art in heofenum,/ gehalgod bi thin name-e, / thin rice be-com to the. . . .*"

"Much better," he admitted. "And I can understand it. Have you another prayer?"

I had to confess my failure to have memorized John's prologue either in the Ango-Saxon or Wycliffite translation, but offered instead one of the early Franciscan poems in Middle English, the first I had memorized (I have modified spelling here to give a better sense of the sound):

> Wynter wakneth al my care-e,
> Nou this leves waxeth bar-e;
> Oft y-sike ant morne- sar-e
> Of this worldes joi,
> Hou it geth al to-nought.

Nou it is ant nou it nis,
Al geth bot Goddes wille,
Al we shal die, that us like yille.

Al that grene me graueth gren-e,
Nou it falweth al bi-den-e;
Jesu! Help that it be sen-e,
For y-not whider y shal
Ne hou lang here dwelle.

He smiled. "*E meglio. Bravo! Mille grazie!*"

There followed a most wonderful conversation about what it means when we say that God hears and answers prayer.

Fra Fernando became a friend, though he didn't think much of Sister Giotto, whom he seemed to have heard of, though not met. "Bah," is all he would say about her when I recounted her role in getting me in touch with his brother.

I spent quite a few hours over the following weeks in the medieval manuscript collection at Convento Ognisanti. In addition to sermons of S. Bernadino da Sienna, I looked at a pastoral handbook of the thirteenth century and read some other sermons. It was a fruitful time. Each day I noticed a friar, Fra Guido Canarozzi, across the room, working away, using journals, and writing down notations. He was a quiet person, shy and yet gracious. He would smile at me, then put his head down and work on at his project. Later I learned that this project was writing defenses of the Catholic position against artificial means of birth control. However, I would soon see him at work in quite another context.

The flood of November 1966 had left a mess everywhere and one could see the high-water mark of the Arno on walls all over the city. Inside courtyards, cloisters, and churches the water had severely damaged important frescoes, altars, and even sculpture. The water took weeks to recede fully, the mud much longer to shovel away. The damage to books, paintings, and frescoes took much, much longer to deal with. My favorite wooden sculpture of any period is Donatello's "Penitent Mary Magdalene," which had been in the baptistery beside the Duomo; it had been so badly damaged by submersion that the restoration team working on it, hidden away from public view, were rumored to think they might never be able to bring it back to anything like its pre-flood condition. In January 1968, when I arrived, most of the effort to recover such artwork and restore it to location was very much still in process. The "Mud Angels," mostly international art students, had in considerable numbers stayed on to work with professional art restorers. I was pleased to discover that some of the *Canadiensi* among them had suggested a method to remove exposed frescoes from walls so that restoration could be attempted in workshops and studios. One had recommended that Masonite, a thin, flexible, durable material in 4-feet by 8-feet sheets, be imported from Canada. These were coated on the smooth side with water-soluble glue and placed right over the discolored and salinated paint surface. Once dry, the fresco and two or three inches of the plaster behind it could be removed from the walls, then in the shop the fresco could be set in a frame box with fresh plaster. When that was dry, the Masonite and water-soluble glue could be removed by soaking the masonite. I saw some of this in process, led around by none other than Sister Giotto. On one such foray she introduced me to Sergio Bertelli, a somewhat too dapper art historian with no single fixed locus of remunerated employment, apparently, but an affiliation with the University and considerable influence. This included his friendship with Piero Bargellini, a scholarly Florentine who had the misfortune of being mayor at the time of the flood. Sergio was pleasant enough, sympathetic that many of the medieval manuscripts I had hoped to read were damaged and still unavailable to users. We had espresso together in a café near Santo Spirito and afterwards walked across the Ponte Santa Trinita. I had been speaking of my interest in the Franciscan-inspired style change of the thirteenth century, from Cimabue through Giotto and on, and its effects from the *Meditationes Vita Christi* into vernacular poetry and song. This prompted him to narrate a story of this style change and its continuing effect at a later date.

"You have seen the crucifix of Brunelleschi in Santa Maria Novella?"

I had yet to see it.

"You must go tomorrow to see it. The Dominicans were more intellectual. Therefore they preferred the older iconic style. This one has a very thin, even emaciated corpus—very good, even moving. But Brunelleschi's friend and rival Donatello thought it also—well—not so good in an important way: after complimenting Brunelleschi, Donatello said, 'This is beautiful work, my friend, but you seem to have forgotten one thing. Christ was also a man. Indeed, he was a *contadino*' (farmer-laborer). There is a story that one day, while Donatello was working on his own wooden crucifix for Santa Croce, Brunelleschi brought a lunch and some eggs to his friend's studio. When the door was opened he saw the nearly finished body in white wood, gasped, and dropped the basket of eggs!"

"Where can I find this story?" I asked. "It's perfect."

"Oh, it is in Vasari. Doubtless apocryphal."

I was disappointed.

"Now, now, David. You are a student of medieval poetry. You should know that the important thing is not that the facts are true, but that what the story *says* is true."

I took the point. Afterward, however, I would discover that Sergio had muddled up the "facts," even as they are presented in Vasari's *Lives of the Artists. Figurati.*

Sister Giotto had recommended to me a fine little trattoria not far from the Adria as a place I should eat lunch. I liked it so much that I became a regular. Sergio, the chief waiter, hung a bottle of wine on a peg over my customary table in the corner by the kitchen, and after a very pleasant *primo* and *secundo* platter I would go to the *signora* at the cash register to pay, and he or she would reach under the counter and pour me a small parting glass of Aliatico, slowing me down a little for a chat.

"You eat much too quickly, Signor Grande," Sergio admonished. "How many fewer pages a day would you read at the Biblioteca Centrale if you took just fifteen more minutes?"

This was a ritual conversation. We both knew that I'd go back to the Adria for siesta and read there before returning to the library.

Hours were fixed at the BNC: access to the collections ceased before noon, and slip orders for new books were not accepted again until 3 p.m. So we laughed as we played out this game, which I finally began to realize was really Sergio's way of helping me improve my Italian.

One day in the midst of it, in came Sister Giotto.

"Hey, David! Listen to Sergio. Besides, if you don't get too much done this year, you have an excuse to come back! This is Firenze. You've got to get over this Protestant work ethic of yours!"

She was with a rather stern-looking woman whose name I can't remember, but as I was leaving, Giotto came out onto the sidewalk after me and said, "What time can you be here for lunch tomorrow? I have a couple of people for you to meet. You'll find them interesting."

We agreed on noon, my usual time.

When I arrived Giotto was already at a table with her guests, a young, well-turned-out woman and a man of about my own age.

"This is Suzy," said Giotto, "and Mahmoud, her boyfriend. David is studying medieval Franciscans, but not painters. Just poets and preachers."

The usual pleasantries followed. After Sergio had taken our order, set *panni* on the table, and poured wine, I learned that Suzy had graduated from Wellesley College and was in Florence on a gap year, taking in art and generally enjoying herself on her family's money. Mahmoud, on the other hand, who spoke broken Italian and bits of English, had come from Iran to study architecture. He was a Bahai, therefore a member of a persecuted minority in Iran, and as I learned later, his official papers were in some disorder or other. He was afraid that if he returned to Tehran to sort things out he wouldn't get another visa to return. He had been attending classes irregularly, not able to afford regular fees, and living in an apparently very marginal condition when Suzy chanced upon him.

"*Si*," admitted Mahmoud, "I had a hotplate and cooked for myself if I caught a pigeon."

"Caught a pigeon?" I asked.

"*Si, piccione.*"

"He was buying seeds—or finding them—and putting them on his window sill. When a pigeon would come, he would reach out quickly and grab it," said Suzy, looking adoringly at her friend. I noticed that Mahmoud was rather fashionably dressed.

"He has very fast hands," she added.

Sister Giotto laughed. "Evidently!"

It further turned out that Suzy, having met him in a piazza as he was sketching the façade of Santa Maria Novella, and learning his story while they ate at a local *ristorante*, had just brought him home to her rather up-scale apartment. That was months before and was now where he lived.

"Suzy is not a Catholic," said Giotto, "or any kind of church-goer for that matter. But we have to admit that she practices charity!"

Everyone laughed, even Mahmoud.

There was some discussion of the Bahai faith, with Mahmoud emphasizing its Zoroastrian roots. Then somehow the subject changed, and Sister Giotto insisted that I walk up the mountain to see San Miniato al Monte at my earliest opportunity.

"The view from there is spectacular," she said.

As we were leaving Artemino's, while Suzy was paying the tab, there were no complimentary glasses of Aliatico, I noticed, and Sergio whispered in my ear before I stepped into the street, "*Ora ha il piccione*" (Now she has the pigeon). He shook his head. It was clear that he had overheard quite a bit of our conversation.

"*Domani, Signor?*"

"*Sì,*" I replied, "*domani.*"

The next day being Friday, the texts I was working on in the Biblioteca would be unavailable in the afternoon, so I resolved to have lunch at Artemino's and then hike up the mountain to see San Miniato. When I got to Artemino's, Sergio was ready to pour me a glass from my basket bottle of Orvieto, and as soon as I had agreed to the *speciale* he sat down across from me.

"Signor, do you know what means "*lei ha l'uccelo in mano? Hai capito?*"

"She has the bird in hand?" I repeated.

"*Non—ma in figura.*" He then went on to explain the vulgar connotations. "It is a joke we have," he said, "not nice, *ma e vera qui.*"

He muttered something I did not understand, followed by an exclamation, "Bah! And that nun: *la suora e pazza.* (The nun is crazy.) *Stai attento, Signor.*"

When I had finished my *pesce* there was a glass of Aliatico already poured for me when I came up to pay my bill. We drank each other's good health.

"*Goditi la tua scalata, Signor!*"

And quite a climb it was, up through narrow streets with clotheslines joining apartments across the gap, many with washed undergarments hanging out to dry. Once past the Pitti Palace and its surroundings you ascend by zigs, zags, stairs, and cobble streets toward the Belvedere, a fort built to help defend the city through its endless wars of the late Middle Ages and Renaissance. I went first to the Belvedere, from which the view both ways—over the city and over the lovely Tuscan hills, rich in vineyards and olive groves—was splendid. The Boboli Gardens are right below, so I was happy to pass through those as well, and, as it was a beautiful late February day, it was nearly 3 p.m. when I reached the base of the great staircase leading up to the basilica. I entered the church, walked around slowly, observing with much appreciation. There had been an early Christian church here, but the present structure was begun a millennium ago (ca. 1018) and gradually brought to completion about the second decade of the thirteenth century. Founded as a Benedictine abbey church, then in the following century influenced by the Cluniacs, the abbey is now home to the Olivetans, a small Italian order that had just recently re-engaged its lost Benedictine roots and Rule (1960). Giotto had insisted that the monks, only eight in number, were the last surviving *convento* of Reformed (White) Benedictines. This was not strictly accurate, but her claim that the monks were aging ("nobody under forty") and that I had better hurry up ("soon they'll be gone") seemed close to the mark. I know this because my heart was heavy that day, and when I saw a small card saying that Vespers, celebrated in the crypt, was "open to worshippers but not to tourists," I made my way down to the crypt. I was entranced to find a marvelous early Romanesque hodgepodge of pillars and stone columns holding up the massive weight above. Large torches in ancient iron brackets were attached to the largest stone columns, lit. There were candles near the altar, also lit.

I sat in the ombré silence, then knelt to pray. As I was praying, eight monks, robed in white and chanting, entered and approached the altar. I was the only other person there. I had no book of the canonical hours but could understand almost enough of the Latin prayers and lections. When the last prayer was ended, with a unison "Amen," I stayed on for a few minutes.

Eventually I went up and out into the cemetery, a surreal blend of pagan and Christian symbolism on its sepulchers and grave markers, some of the more recent of which, especially in the columbarium, had photos of the deceased under glass.

Somewhat bewildered, and tired as well, I sat to rest and ponder on a bench behind the apse. I continued praying, with my head in my hands. At last I sat up, becoming aware that it would take me some time to get back, then to get ready for dinner with new friends. Before I could stand, a white sleeve and hand extended through a niche in the stone wall of the church, and made a sign of the cross over me before withdrawing, mysteriously, whence it came.

"*Deo gratias. Alleluia, alleluia.*"
I walked down toward the Arno, these words running over and over in my mind.

I got into the habit of going up to San Miniato al Monte for Vespers.

As time went on, I spent evenings and Saturdays with many of the people Giotto had made part of my world—soccer-playing, boar-hunting, macho friends of Sergio Mariotti, and others—but I saw less and less of Sister Giotto herself. In fact, I made some effort to minimize my participation in her familiar circles. This was not because I didn't laugh at her jokes; it was to some degree because I *did* laugh at her jokes. Then later I would feel bad about it.

The bravura and ribald worldliness of the soccer club, the ridiculous overindulgences of food and drink at places like the Gia Rosta, the *grappa* drinking contests, seemed to me decidedly less problematic. No one was pretending to virtue in those environs. On the other hand, in my memory most of those men now seem less distinct as individuals; they tend to blend into one another. In short, though they were often "over the top" in their behavior, they lacked the appeal to me of the real characters I met in other places, such as the crazy operatic singing barbers, Luigi and Enrico, and some of the patrons of their shop where I went for a haircut. While it is at first disconcerting to have a burly man with a razor roaring in your ear the *aria* "After grief one is more content, after pain one is happier" (from Monteverdi's *La favola d'Orfeo*), within a few visits that sort of entertainment became rather delightful in its way. Almost always I heard a new *aria*, and sometimes from Enrico, the older barber, a recitative. I marveled that these working-class, modestly-educated men had far deeper musical knowledge and talent than I did. Giotto had once persuaded me to go with her and a group of her friends to a performance of Beethoven's *Fidelio* at the opera house. It had been excellent, and with the accoutrement of bouquets of roses flying stage-ward at the end—well, clichéd also. The barbershop was better in some ways.

This brings me to another person I regard as most certainly "real," and one who had an abiding impact on my memory and gratitude. Amadea was a house cleaner in the Adria, a tiny woman in her sixties, always cheerful. She went about her duties in the halls, foyer, lounge and breakfast room singing arias too, from *Carmen*, Monteverdi's *Arianna*, even from Puccini's *Madame Butterfly*. When I would see her she would smile broadly and say, "*Scusi, Signor Grande* (she was not more than four and half feet tall). *Ti displace se canto?*" Because of her Abruzzese accent I thought at first she was asking me if I also would sing. I answered "*no, Signora*," which worked well, for truly, I not only didn't mind her singing; I enjoyed it.

By April it had become my method to work through notes I had acquired from my stint in the libraries and begin to order them toward my dissertation project. This meant that I would spend much of the day at the desk in my room. With the window open, I could see across the inner court to the kitchen. Occasionally Amadea would wave to me and I would wave back. As Easter approached, I found myself also working late, concerned that I would not get everything in order before having to return to Princeton. It was thus, late on Saturday, April 13 of that year, that I was writing draft text when suddenly there came a knock at my door. It was Amadea.

"*Buona Pascha! Buona Pascha, Signor Grande!*"

I returned her greeting, of course, but observed that it was still Saturday.

"*E quasi mezanotte! Venire! Vieni, unisciti a noi!*"

She beckoned vigorously for me to follow her. Unorthodox as this midnight invitation was, I followed her down the hall, then down a flight of stairs by the breakfast room to the kitchen, where I was introduced to two other women, a larger one in her fifties, I guessed, and a somewhat younger woman, both of whom I had only seen from across the courtyard, working kitchen and laundry. All smiled, and pointed to a massive bottle of Asti Spumante on the metal surface of the kitchen work island. There were four glasses. I was motioned to one of the stools, and Amadea poured all glasses, then made this toast: "*Alla bellisima Risurrezione di nostro Signor!*"

There was some happy, lively conversation, a lot of which I could not follow, except so far as to understand that the two older women especially were devout Catholics.

Finally I asked a question I had been wanting to ask for some time, but when I made the effort with Sister Giotto, it had been the occasion of a dismissive joke about my "Protestant seriousness."

"How is it, Signora Amadea, that when I go to churches on Sunday morning I see very few people in attendance? There are churches and priests everywhere in Firenze, but there seem to be very few people who are really Catholic, no?"

"Ah, but it is not so that just because you see few in the churches that many more are not seriously Catholic," she replied.

Her answer was beginning to seem to me similar to Sister Giotto's, in fact, when suddenly she added, "*Dio ama coloro che lo adorano in spiritu e verita*" (God loves those who worship him in spirit and truth). "One does not need always a church for that."

It was a party of only fifteen minutes duration or so (why aren't there more parties like that?) but I returned to my room comforted and lifted up in heart. I have never forgotten Amadea (whose name means "lover of God") nor that very remarkable Easter morning.

We were not out of the octave of Easter when a terrible thing happened in the kitchen of the Adria. The proprietors of the pensione, Luciano and Diana Zucconi, who I had by this time gotten to know pretty well, had two children, a girl about eight or nine at the time, and a six-year old boy named Ricci. Ricci was a bit of a mischief, full of energy, always running around the halls. One Friday afternoon, shortly after lunch, Ricci zoomed around a corner and into the kitchen, just in time to knock into the cook, Theresa, as she was lifting a large pot of scalding hot soup off the stove. A lot of it, I learned, had spilled on Ricci, burning him badly.

I was just finishing my lunch when Diana burst into Artemino's crying, "Is David here?"

She saw me rise and came to me breathlessly.

"Ricci has been burned. He has gone to the hospital in an ambulance. I cannot find Luciano anywhere. They will not treat him unless they are first paid. Please come!" All this was a great deal less coherent than I have made it sound. Amadea had told her where likely to find me (fortunately, I had not left for San Miniato yet) and she had gone with Ricci in the ambulance. Diana, in a frenzy of anxiety, left as suddenly as she had arrived, yelling out the name of the hospital, which I did not catch. But Sergio had written it down, along with an easy map of how to get there. "You pay next time," he said. "Go!"

I ran. Santa Maria Nuova is not that far, but I was drenched in sweat when I got there. It was very difficult to get helpful answers as to how to find Ricci. At length I was shown up a set of stairs, and as I climbed I could hear a child screaming in pain. Ricci was on a gurney in the hall. Diana was beside him—no one else.

"Have they looked at him?" I asked, over the child's howling.

"No. Here they demand payment first. That's why I needed Luciano."

As a graduate student of modest means I was alarmed that Diana clearly hoped I could solve the problem, but as I learned from the business office, I had not the means to do so. They would not take my last few American Express travellers checks, let alone the card. They wanted *lira* in an amount far beyond my means. Argument was fruitless. They wouldn't let me sign a promissory note or offer a check on my bank in Princeton.

"Are you the father?" snapped the orderly.

"No! I am a visiting student."

"Sorry. We must have [I think it was] 50,000 *lira* before we can put him in a room."

I went back upstairs to where Ricci was still crying loudly and Diana sobbing beside him. She was disconsolate when I told her of my failure.

"They are monsters!" she almost shouted.

I looked down at Ricci. His shoulders and arms were purple, and there were blisters. He couldn't bear the weight of the sheet. It was awful.

Just then a nurse and the orderly appeared, with Luciano right behind them. Amadea had found him (I never learned where). Ricci was wheeled into a room and the nurse gave him a pill. The boy kept on crying incessantly. No doctor appeared for nearly an hour. Once there, he examined Ricci's arms, shoulders, and chest.

"Very severe burns," he said, and left.

That was all the help he got, other than a glass of water, for the next hour. Luciano's father and mother arrived, and like the rest of us, stood helplessly looking on as Ricci wailed. By then it was past four o'clock, and this had been going on since noon.

Just then the door opened and a nurse showed in a tiny man in a brown cassock, belted with a rope with three knots. He looked at me and smiled briefly before going straight to Ricci's bedside. It was Fra Guido Canarozzi.

Bending over the crying child, he made a sign of the cross and whispered something inaudible to me. It seemed to be a question, and Ricci said some incoherent words in response through his tears. Fra Guido spoke quietly to Ricci, too quietly for me to hear, then began praying. Suddenly it occurred to us all, with huge relief, that Ricci had stopped crying. There was more brief conversation between the child and the friar, then another prayer.

"Ricci is smiling!" exclaimed Diana. And he was. Fra Guido straightened up, made one more sign of the cross over Ricci, and then smiling to the rest of us, said, *"Buona serra, amici.* It will be better now." Then, with a nod my way, he left and the door to the room closed behind him.

It was stunning. To this day I have not seen anything like it. Diana was talking with Ricci, and Luciano's father turned to me and said, "I hate priests. I spit on the ground when they pass. But if there are any who know God, it is these *cappucini."*

Papa Zucconi, I knew, had been an ardent *fascisti.* His cousin, Gabriel d'Annunzio, the poet, was a famous adherent of Mussolini. Luciano had been raised as a *piccolo Musselini* in strident anti-clericalism, and none of them went to church even at Easter. Knowing all this made Papa Zucconi's confession all the more remarkable.

Still more remarkable is what I learned the next morning from Diana. Though I left within a half hour or so of Fra Guido, having an appointment at a café to confer with a curator from the library, apparently some time after that another doctor had come into Ricci's room. He examined him and said, "Where are the burns?"

Normal color had returned to Ricci's body. There were no blisters visible. This doctor was plainly irritated, and immediately ordered discharge, much to Diana's relief. Ricci had been sent home, reconciled with the cook, and gone to bed and slept peacefully. He even made a shy appearance to thank me "for helping" before going off to play the next morning.

"It is as though nothing happened," sighed Diana. "But we saw the horrible burns," I replied. "And yes, heard him screaming all those hours," said Diana. "You knew the Franciscan, didn't you? How did you let him know?"

"I didn't. I think he was just making his rounds at the hospital," I said quietly.

"It was a miracle," said Diana. "That's what Amadea says."

"I believe her. You should too, I think. And ask Amadea about such things. I bet she will tell you that such miracles come from God."

As it happened, I never saw Fra Guido again, sadly, for I surely wanted to. He had gone to Rome when I last visited Convento Ognisanti, only a week or so before heading back to Princeton. I had wanted to thank many people, including more than a few not mentioned here, who had hosted me to dinner and been part of my rich experience in Firenze. I made up a list, including the friars Fernando and Guido, found a Chinese restaurant I could afford, and in all twenty-two people came. But neither friar. They gave us a long table. I was at one end, Sister Giotto with Suzy and Mahmoud at the other. Sergio Mariotti and Marta were in the middle, opposite Luciano and Diana. Carolyn Valone and Judy Chidester sat opposite Libby and Francesco Buttazzi, and so on. Most folks already knew each other, and everybody, of course, knew Sister Giotto. It was a wonderful, merry evening. I knew something even then about Chinese cooking from some fellow graduate students at Princeton and surprised the waiter by asking if they ever made *joudsa*, for I couldn't find them on the menu. She seemed delighted; running off to the kitchen she soon returned with the chef, also Chinese.

"You know *joudsa?*" he asked in Chinese.

"I love them," I replied in Italian.

"Well then I shall make *joudsa* for you as well," she beamed, "compliments of the house."

To that point in my life I had never paid such a restaurant bill, and it used up almost all my remaining American Express travelers checks to manage it, but it was worth it.

Giotto had evidently drunk quite a lot by the time it was her turn to say goodbye. I never saw her again either—the next April, when I returned to Florence for a few months, she was not to be found at the Gonzaga Institute, and I never did get a clear answer as to why. (I have since heard that she was recalled by her order and sent to a convent in Arizona.) In any case, I was pressing hard by then to turn my doctoral dissertation into a book, and living as a house guest in the *castello* where now resided Luciano and Diana with their family. I touched bases with many of my former male friends, the friars of Ognisanti included, but otherwise did all I could to redeem precious library time before heading back in mid-August. As I was preparing to leave, I found myself reflecting that I owed Sister Giotto a good deal for her many introductions to interesting people, but that my most persistent gratitude was likely to be for folks she never knew, like Amadea, Fra Guido, Fra Fernando, and the nameless Olivetan monks of San Miniato al Monte, whose Vespers I still managed often to attend, a solitary *stranieri* from a far country.

PHILIP AND THE TWO JACKS

ONE OF THE PRIVILEGES of being a faculty member or fellow of a British university is eating in the Senior Common Room. When I was Reckett and Coleman Visiting Professor at the University of Hull in 1970–71, I was glad of the access. Some of my colleagues ate there frequently. The food tended to be mushy, starchy, and sodden with brown gravy, but the bar offered several good Yorkshire ales on tap, including Younger's No. 3. At the beginning of Michelmas term I would sometimes indulge in a half-pint with my liver and kidney pie, especially on days on which I had no lectures after lunch.

On one occasion the theologian A.T. Hanson and his brother, a physicist, called me to their table to introduce me to the librarian, Philip Larkin. With his bald pate, horn-rimmed glasses, tweed jacket, tie and weskit, Philip looked the part. He was cordial and invited me to call on him if I needed any help with the medieval collection. He clearly knew at least that much about me, which I found pleasantly surprising.

A couple of weeks later I happened to be finishing up just as the librarian came from the bar along with a chap I would learn was the historian John Kenyon, each with full pints in hand.

"Ah, Jeffrey," said he. "If you can spare the time, why don't you get a proper pint and come join us in the lounge? I'd like you to meet another of our colleagues."

I was willing, and fetched my pint of Younger's No. 3. When I got to where they were, the three regulars were comfortably ensconced in gentlemen's club style leather chairs. They motioned me to a fourth armchair and I sat.

"Jeffrey, these are my friends, Jack Kenyon and Jack Watt, both historians. Gentlemen, Jeffrey is the "Mustard Professor" this year, from Rochester in the United States. But you are in fact a Canadian, are you not?"

We exchanged greetings, and all raised pints in my direction when I admitted to my citizenship. I raised mine in return.

"Younger's No. 3 by the color," said Kenyon. "Good choice."

John Phillips Kenyon, aka "Jack," had been a doctoral student of the renowned J.H. Plumb at Cambridge, and a fellow at Cambridge for several years before coming to Hull as Head of the History Department. He knew more about the Stuarts and seventeenth century England than anyone I ever met, and was by then one of the most highly respected historians in Britain. In person he was all Yorkshireman—brusque, blunt-spoken, and hardy as a good horse.

Jack Watt, a professor of matters medieval, was far less distinguished, though well-liked by his students. He was a whimsical, soft-spoken, almost timid man of slight build and, as I began to learn, of sometimes astonishing naivete or perhaps guilelessness.

"We have a soft spot for Canadians," he said. "Since the War especially."

He was referring to WWII. When I mentioned that my father and seven of my uncles had served along with the British forces in army, navy and air force, there immediately ensued what would be an enduring topic of our conversation all through that academic year. Each of them remembered the bombing, Watt in Belfast, the other two in Coventry and London. My comparative youth and lack of comparable experience made me a listener; I asked a few questions and learned a lot.

Philip was first and foremost an ardent Englishman. In his estimation, Britain was in rapid decline since the loss of Churchill. He reviled the Germans, but scorned the French and Italians even more, sometimes quite openly. It was some weeks of Tuesday lunches, at which they insisted I become a regular, before I learned that Philip was something more than the University Librarian.

"You don't have much about the war in your poems," observed Watt.

"If you knew how to read them, Jack, you might see it everywhere," said Philip softly.

"Poems?" I blurted it out.

"You don't know that Philip is also a poet?" Kenyon set his near empty pint on the side table. "His disguise is evidently enough to fool an English professor too!" He laughed.

I was embarrassed.

"It hasn't ever come up before," I protested lamely. I wouldn't have guessed."

"Well," said Philip, rather dourly, "you won't need to worry about it here. It is one of our rules. We talk about many things, but poetry and poets are absolutely excluded."

Kenyon jumped in. "Watt slipped there."

That was all that was said about it then, or ever afterward. We all got up, and I for my part went straight to the bookstore and purchased a copy of *The Less Deceived*, a tidy little volume which I still have and value highly. It is a very fine collection of acutely perceived and trenchantly realized poems.

The next Tuesday I wondered if I would be so welcome to the company of Philip and the two Jacks. As it happened, Philip saw me as he was heading for a pint, and sang out, "See you in a moment, David." It was the first time he had used my given name. Relieved, I got my pint and joined the group.

"Are you interested in music?" asked Philip. I was happy to say yes.

"What about jazz?"

"Very much so," I replied. "In high school I was part of a band. We played a lot of New Orleans style jazz."

I could hardly have said anything better.

"Philip's favorite topic," said Watt. "Be careful. He knows more about jazz than Dizzie Gillespie."

Everyone laughed. It turned out that Philip had a massive collection of vinyl LPs and had even written some newspaper columns on individual artists and movements. His knowledge was prodigious. When he went home to his flat at the end of the day he would pour himself a gin and tonic and "saturate himself" (Kenyon's phrase) with Count Basie, Louis Armstrong, Duke Ellington, Dizzie Gillespie (a favorite), Dave Brubeck, Bessie Smith, and Ella Fitzgerald. He was a true fan, but also a professional critic who had reviewed jazz albums from 1961 to the time I knew him. He quipped that this was largely so he could get the free LPs. He also played the saxophone tolerably well, according to Kenyon, though "you had to get him pretty well sauced in his own flat to persuade him to play."

"There's nothing better than a good drink and some real jazz to wrap up a dull day," Philip said more than once.

"Ah, and you don't have a wife to complain about it either," said Watt. Watt was married and took some teasing for being henpecked. Philip, as I did not know then, had a series of romantic involvements but avoided making any commitment to marriage. One of my English Department colleagues speculated that he was secretly gay, but nothing could have been further from the truth. I asked if he had read the first poem in *The Less Deceived*, a volume dedicated to his most perdurable amour, Monica Jones. He hadn't.

"I think it is one of the most touching British love poems of the twentieth century," I replied, "and certainly heterosexual."

How come he never married then?" asked another slow bunny. "Ask him for yourself," I replied, and walked away. Truth to tell, all a person had to do was read his poems. Philip was just as he portrayed himself, not only afraid to make that abiding commitment but constrained even in contemplating it because he genuinely felt that it would be unfair to ask someone into his life who might thereby become depressed with his own disenchantment. Critics often assign him a debt to T.S. Eliot but fail to note how the kind of peace in solitariness exhibited by Hopkins was more apt. In rejecting the notion that couples are happier than singles, he dubs it

Inaccuracy, as far as I am concerned.
What calls me is that lifted, rough-tongued bell
(Art, if you like) whose individual sound
Insists I too am an individual.
It speaks; I hear; others may hear as well.

The final sestet of Hopkins' sonnet "Kingfishers catch fire" is not, of course, affirmed, but there is irony in this Hopkins allusion in the penultimate stanza of his "Reasons for Attendance," a poem that says, in effect, "to each his own." In this as in other respects, Philip was entirely consistent.

"Have you ever heard Oscar Peterson live?" Philip asked me once. He was clearly disappointed that at that point I had to admit that I hadn't.

"Now, Philip," said Kenyon, "you haven't heard many of your favorites live either. What would you do without the BBC and your collection?"

"You know I don't like crowds," huffed Philip.

That certainly seemed true. It wasn't just that poetry was off-limits. I learned that he refused to give public readings, even in England. He had been invited to America to read but refused. In fact, he had never traveled outside of England and had no intention of doing so.

I asked him once if he would ever consider taking a temporary post as a visiting librarian, say at the University of Rochester.

"I would not go to the United States."

"How about Canada?"

A longer pause. "I don't know," he said. "I have sometimes thought that if ever I did travel outside the UK the only two places I would consider, really, might be Canada or New Zealand."

When later, from the University of Victoria when I was Chair, I tried to arrange such an offer, he respectfully declined. This is a man who in 1968 was awarded the Order of the British Empire but declined it, and in 1984 was offered the position of Poet Laureate and declined that. As he said, he didn't like crowds and he hated ceremonies. I was disappointed but by then hardly surprised.

Once, when we were all at a Faculty Senate dinner, dressed in our bib and ticker formals and comfortably sipping cognac and smoking the cigars brought to us in silver boxes, I remarked to Philip that we hadn't quite arrived at a comparable level of creature comforts in any place I had previously worked.

"Placebos," he said. "Those you don't pay a living wage to you placate by whatever means you can. Not that I mind these means," he added. He was well aware of his own predilection for the high style, and he was capable of the off-color jokes such an atmosphere tends to provoke. Nonetheless, he was offended when, in his public remarks, Vice-Chancellor Sir Brynmor-Jones belatedly welcomed me as the Reckett and Coleman Visiting Professor. The chief executives of the company were present to be duly thanked as well, but when the Vice-Chancellor referred to me jokingly as "the wild Colonial boy," Philip winced.

"I am sorry," he said, "that was beastly."

(To be fair, it had taken me only a few weeks at Hull to acquire a reputation for unorthodoxy. I insisted on students reading the text *before* coming to the lecture hall, rather than, as was their custom, coming to hear what the professor would say before reading the texts. The scandalized students' complaints were apparently well distributed.)

Occasionally former colleagues of my Tuesday lunch friends were a subject of conversation or just fond recollection. Kenyon asked me if I had ever heard of Decima Douie. Indeed I had, had read some of her work on the early Franciscans, and had tremendous admiration for her book on Archbishop John Peckham.

"Well, you'd have found her worth your time over tea," said Watt. "She had enormous knowledge, and was generous with it."

"Not to mention that she, along with Ray Brett [Head of English Language and Literature], was the driving force on the committee which brought us Philip," added Kenyon.

"And she is the reason you are finding the medieval literature collection as good as it is," said Philip. "She would bring me an envelope filled with slips of paper on which she had written full bibliographic details for books. She would say, 'Philip, we simply *must* have these," then wend her way promptly back into the stacks.'"

"Now, now, Philip. You would often make her a cup of tea."

Philip laughed. "Well, yes. And despite her trying, betimes a bit too much, to convert me, she was an unfailingly interesting mind."

"Well, she is a giant of a scholar," I said. "When did she leave Hull for Oxford?"

"When she retired. When was it, Jack?" Philip turned to Kenyon, who had been her colleague.

"In 1967," he replied. "She had loved Oxford as a student, and was a great friend of Beryl Smalley [another outstanding medievalist]. But it makes me laugh to think of you calling her a giant. I take it you've never met her."

"No, though I would like to."

"Well, you'll have to look down a long way," said Philip. "And be careful. She isn't a lot bigger than your briefcase."

Watt then recalled seeing her waiting at a bus stop one windy day, when suddenly a gust bowled her head over heels like a tumbleweed. She refused to let go of her umbrella and was utterly indignant when helped to her feet. It sounded a bit like a scene from Winnie the Pooh. "Mad as a wet hen," Watt added. "Smallest adult woman I have ever seen, but mighty in spirit. A real force of nature, that woman."

"I've always wondered why anyone with a name like Douie would name their child Decima, and even so, give her the middle name beginning with an 'L.' What does it stand for?"

"Well, she was the tenth and final child of Sir James Douie," said Philip, laughing, "and in his whimsy he gave her the middle name Langworthy, a reference I think to a family connection." Philip was a font of information on distinguished families of the past, as I would learn, often to my amusement.

It has been sometimes said of Philip that his reclusive disdain for public honors, even public readings of his poetry, was something of a stage persona. I do not think so; one should distinguish between firm principles, even or perhaps especially when they are against the grain of societal norms, and the carefully manicured affectations of someone who cultivates a public image. To those who knew him well, Philip was certainly cynical about some notions of honor, selectively reclusive, but at heart a most amiable fellow, utterly dependable, unpretentious with his friends, and often quite funny. Indeed, he just preferred a few regular friends to being "hail fellow" with many acquaintances. He may have been something of a melancholic, but he cherished a pint, a chat, and a good laugh.

His closest friends, save his erstwhile amours, were the two Jacks. Kenyon, utterly competent and that rarest of creatures, an intelligent monarchist, was closer certainly than Watt, but Philip loved "little Jack" as once he called him, not in spite of his incompetencies but almost because of them. Jack Watt was guileless. Let me close with an account of something quite wonderful that happened to which I became inadvertently privy.

Jack Watt lived just off campus, right across the street from a women's dormitory. One night after he had gone to bed, he heard a nightingale singing in one of the trees next to that building. He was a "birder," as they called folk who were amateur ornithologists there, and wanted to register a sighting. Still in his pajamas, he went out with a flashlight, and started shining it up into the trees along the building. It was thus, he told us, that when the local constabulary apprehended him, they misunderstood him when he said, "Honestly, I'm just trying to spot a bird."

"Right," said the constable, who seemed to understand Watt's word in a much less innocent colloquial sense. "And no identification, eh? Well fortunately we spotted you first. Come with us."

At the station Jack was equally unsuccessful with his alibi. They were in the process of booking him when he asked if he could call home. No one answered. He pled to make another call, to Kenyon, then realized his friend was away at a conference. He tried Philip, who was a bit sauced and had fallen asleep listening to jazz, but agreed to come to the station, bringing identification. Philip gave surety, and drove the bewildered Jack home.

Telling it all to Kenyon and me over an extra pint of Younger's No. 3, Philip was a wonderful narrator. Poor Jack was painfully embarrassed. And then Philip said something that revealed to me Larkin's true character.

"Ah, it's alright, Jack," he said. "We'll have a good laugh over this for a long time. Actually, it's rather splendid to know someone so pure in heart as Jack Watt. I'd go bail you out anytime."

Philip remains in my memory as an unusual but cherishable short-term friend. We had in religious affections virtually nothing in common, but I regard him as spiritually perceptive. His poem "Church Going" is usually read, not unreasonably, as his expression of distancing from formal Christian faith. But it is also the most prescient prophecy of the dismal fate of the Church of England of his time. Not all prophets are believers, and very few indeed are insiders. Philip qualified in both respects—outside looking in, but seeing more than those caught up in the dance.

ALTON MCKEEVER

THE STORY ABOUT ALTON McKeever's big Holstein bull and the road surveyor was McKeever's signature narrative long before Katherine and I moved, lock, stock, barrel, cattle, and machinery, to Windhover Farm, near Spencerville, Ontario, in 1988. Alton McKeever's farm was across the road, and after it winds its way out of Limerick Forest and through our farm, Indian Creek flows under the County Road bridge and down through McKeever's place to the Nation River. McKeever's fences were in terrible shape; his miserable, scruffy cattle often got out on the road, and once came up under the bridge and into our pastures. We had an ugly time separating them out from our herd and back to whence they came. More than once a number of us neighbors had to round up his cattle from the road almost all the way to Roebuck, not to mention hold off traffic until we could get them back home. Never once did McKeever himself appear, and no manner of entreaties could get him to repair his rusted, patchwork barbed wire fences. The Ontario Provincial Police had been called more than once, to no avail. McKeever was pretty much the epitome of a bad neighbor. None of this, however, is part of the story everybody loves to tell about him. That happened several years before we came to live across the road.

It seems that the County Road office wanted to widen the shoulders and deepen the ditches on the stretch between Spencerville and Roebuck. The reason given for this decision was typical; in years of heavy snow there wasn't quite enough margin both to keep the surface reasonably clear and get the snow out and deep enough into the ditches that the roads wouldn't drift over again ten minutes after the plows had passed. While there was to be no change to the road allowance itself (66 feet in total–33 feet from each side of the crown of the blacktop), they needed to redo the road survey for the first time in nearly a century. Generally speaking, road widening is a benefit to farmers, because even though the new survey might cost them a few feet of pasture here and there, the county would install better culverts and a new fence-line gratis, presumably to avoid legal troubles but unofficially to express their appreciation for landowner cooperation.

On a sunny day in May, Alton McKeever looked out his kitchen window to see a white government pickup truck coming up his lane. He wasn't pleased. Swinging open the door, he reportedly uttered a blast of profanity in the midst of which charges of trespassing and aspersions regarding the driver's ancestry seem to have been included. Nevertheless, the surveyor stepped out and indicated his business.

"We are fixing the road," he said, "and when we do that we need to survey to get it right. You'll get a new fence out of it."

"Hell, no!" McKeever replied. "Get off my land!"

The surveyor said something about having the authority to be there and to make his request. "Authority?" snorted McKeever. "What the %#&% is that? On a man's own land?"

The road surveyor reached into his truck and pulled out a clipboard with a paper bearing the county seal as well as another from the Ontario Department of Transport. McKeever stared at these for a minute, then at the emblem on the door of the surveyor's truck, and finally grumbled, "Okay, since you have your damned authority, what do you want to do with it?"

"I just need to go into your front pasture and take a few readings. Shouldn't take me more than half an hour."

"Then, dammit, get on with it."

The surveyor pulled out a transit and tripod from the back of his truck. Wearing his orange vest with the large fluorescent yellow 'X' on the back, and carrying his equipment, he went through the lane gate into McKeever's pasture, set up his tripod at the high end of the field, and began to take sightings. What he didn't see was McKeever going up and into his barn to let his bull—a monstrous Holstein—out and into the pasture. The bull, of course, spied the surveyor, fixed his dull but angry eye on the 'X,' and charged right at it. Just in the nick of time the man saw his doom coming and ran for all his worth, transit and tripod akimbo, for the fence. He scarcely made it. Then he heard McKeever yelling at him from up by the barn, "Show him your authority, dammit!" and laughing like the madman he was.

In order to fetch his tripod, which did not make it over the fence, the surveyor had to call a co-worker on his CB radio and get him, once he came, to distract the bull enough that the surveyor, now *sans gilette*, could reach through the fence and pull the equipment out.

I first heard this little narrative about authority and power from a supply priest when we were between rectors at St. James, Crystal Rock, Anglican Church. There was no name attached. Later on I heard it from several different sources, and in these cases McKeever was identified. It seems that after their bizarre adventure the surveyors retired to the bar in the Spencerville Hotel. One of Henry Kelso's lads and a son of Mick McGuire the sawyer (sadly enough) had pretty much what you might call fulltime jobs there, and they were pretty well into it when the surveyors ordered their first beers. They got the story. From thence it travelled pretty quickly. Apparently someone got the nerve to ask McKeever himself when he saw him in the LCBO (government liquor store). "You really did that?"

"Damn right I did. If the bull had got 'im, would have served him right."

Now in Alton's favor, it should be said, he had a longstanding grudge against officialdom, on account of some federal archaeologists fencing off a chunk of his land along the creek for the sake of the old Iroquois village site there, abandoned fifteen hundred years ago, long before any settlers came. Not in his favor, however, was his perpetual inebriation; no one I knew claimed to have ever seen him sober, and he had let his farm go to rack and ruin because of it. His act of defiance was rewarded by the government *not* giving him a new fence, a fact that all of his neighbors regretted for many years. Authority generally has its way over power in the end, but not always to everyone's satisfaction.

LOUIS BOISVENUE

LOUIS WAS EASILY THE most popular person in and around Spencerville, Ontario, where for many years he had owned and operated an auto repair shop. Louis didn't just fix cars, trucks, and smaller tractors; he also made everyone who knew him feel just a little bit better about the world. Every day, Monday to Saturday, from the time he opened up at 7 a.m. until around 9 a.m., when he turned off the coffee pot and went to work on one or another vehicle in his two-bay garage, his office was filled with locals—anywhere between eight and ten farmers, truckers, and retired men. "Louie's Cultural Center," as Herb Thompson dubbed it, was the place where people exchanged stories, shared news, and enjoyed coffee and lots of jovial laughter. Louis provided the coffee; others took turns bringing donuts or maybe brownies from home.

Part of the reason "Louie," as he and everyone else pronounced his name, was so well liked was his irrepressible sense of humor. He had a perpetual grin and mischievous twinkle in his eyes. He had seen some hard times, including a heart attack at twenty-nine years of age. The doctor wanted him to stop smoking, but of course he didn't. Louis' place reeked so strongly of cigarette smoke that Katherine complained of it on my clothes when I came home. But he never talked about personal hardship—the trials and tribulations of other folks were more than enough to concern him, he said. Infallibly cheerful, he made us all see the bright side of situations.

"Hey, it could always be worse, Dave," he said one day after I had spent much of the night trying to deliver a calf, only to lose it. "Consider Lucky there," he laughed, pointing to a big poster he kept on the wall: "LOST DOG. Black with white chest and face. THREE LEGS, BLIND IN ONE EYE. CASTRATED. MIGHT HAVE FLEAS. ANSWERS TO LUCKY."

A bit later I clipped a report from one of my cattlemen magazines, a verbatim letter to the Canadian National Railroad:

> One of yer locomotives hit my red bull. Broke his hip and mashed his equipment. His hip is some better, but all he can do now is stand around. For a red bull he sure is looking pretty dam blue. I want a thousand dollars compensation.

Louis laughed and posted it beside his "Lucky" poster. "Now that's better. See what I mean, Dave? It could always be worse!"

People with French names were few and far between in South Dundas County then. His family had come two generations earlier, and his mother and father were irregular Catholics. Louis had been baptized, I learned, but hadn't been to church much except for weddings and funerals in a long time when I got to know him in the late 1980s. The affable and unusually popular young priest at St. Lawrence O'Toole parish also liked Louis, and stopped in for coffee a number of times, but he made no headway in getting him to Mass. Louis would just laugh and say, "Now Fr. Rob, you wouldn't want the likes of me showing up at Mass. People would be wondering either if I was taken sick or if you were up to something! Besides, you've got a whole lot of people going now, more than in years around here, and I might just put a jinx on the whole thing!"

There was a large house on the main street between Louis' garage and the Bank building on the corner. It had been bought by a Chinese fellow, a Buddhist, who started up the Sichuan Happy Garden restaurant on the premises. Katherine and I went there a few times, and liked it well enough. So I asked Louis one day if he had ever tried the place out for lunch.

"Actually, I did." Big grin. "Spicy. Odd food. And weird. You get up afterward, then a couple of farts later you're ready to eat lunch all over again—somewhere else." Everyone present laughed. Louis could make even a bad review light-hearted.

Louis' rejection of the Church into which he had been born—and of which he practiced more virtues than most regulars—was more than a passing curiosity to me, and, as later I learned, to Fr. Rob as well. Louis was the most generous, kind-hearted soul anyone could name. Much of what he did was invisible to all but those who experienced it. Not only were his prices more than fair for everyone, he would often fix cars for people hard-up for cash—single moms, men who had lost their jobs—and charge them nothing or next to nothing. Word like that gets around. He was a wiry little man, and could be tough as nails if someone who could well afford to pay were to try to take advantage of him, but everyone in the community that I knew had stories about his coming out to their place late at night or in terrible weather to get them up and running. I was getting by on pretty dubious vehicles at the time, so I had first-hand knowledge.

One of his acts of kindness was, however, apparent to all. Beanie Ferguson was a lad in his late twenties, in some respects quite intellectually challenged, and known for his troubles with excessive drinking and the law. Of uncertain paternity, he lived with his birth mother, and occasionally helped with crop harvesting, but was otherwise mostly unemployed. He was regarded by many as a 'sad case,' socially awkward and always at loose ends. He had suffered taunting in school from peers who called him "Pinto" on account of his bi-color skin and close-cropped, curly hair, tinted with red. He had the typical African flat nose, wide nostrils, and thick lips. Louis had defended him more than once before he took him on as a helper, and he paid him standard wages whilst teaching Beanie how to fix flats, rotate tires, and fetch him tools as he needed them when working head down in an engine or under an exhaust system. We all understood, yet marveled how Louie could keep humoring poor Beanie and encouraging him, even when he made a mess of things or forgot to show up at work until noon. It cannot have been a paying proposition for Louis, but for more than three years it kept Beanie pretty much off the streets and out of trouble. After Beanie decided to move back on to public assistance, their financial relationship ended, but Beanie never forgot to mention Louis' generosity to him and frequently stopped by for a visit.

We were all talking about names in his shop one morning—why some people were called Taylor or Baker or Smith—and I suggested that maybe some of his Boisvenue ancestors had been loggers. "Could be, but that's not the way we think of it," he said with a laugh. "Maybe it means that we just came out of the bush, either before or after the chimpanzees." Another laugh. "My mother has a theory that it refers to what we don't have between our ears. We were none of us too smart, lad, that's for sure!"

Actually, Louis had never finished high school. And he didn't have a regular mechanic's license, since he didn't take the courses for that either. That's the reason, he would say, he felt he should charge less. But he was the best mechanic for at least thirty miles in any direction.

Louis did people a world of good, but he never pretended to be anything other than the county mischief. Almost every November first, All Saints Day, there would be a hay wagon or some piece of farm machinery atop the flat roof of the Bank of Montreal down on the corner. The culprits never seemed to be apprehended. One such All Saints' Day morning I popped in to the shop for a coffee and visit and observed that it would be a marvel if somebody like Louis didn't have some idea of who was putting that equipment up there. Louis just grinned and said, "Could be I help them, Dave." And laughed. Over his shoulder I noticed two sets of block-and-tackle winches hanging on the wall.

Last October we were back in the Valley for the first time in nearly twenty years, just to see old friends. We stayed a couple of days with my old high school friends, Stan and Penny Reid, and Stan and I went around to see Louis. He had retired and sold his garage, but then decided he needed to put up a smaller two-bay garage next to his house. When we walked in the smoke was thick as ever, and several men were sitting around, chatting with Louis.

"Well if it isn't David Jeffrey," he said with a grin. "I heard you might be in the neighborhood." We stayed for an hour, chatted about life. I had brought him a bottle of Texas hot sauce. "Don't put too much of that stuff on your spaghetti all at once, Louis," I warned. "You might need to change your muffler."

As Stan and I finally got set to leave, I looked at the twenty-year old car Louis was working on. I didn't need to ask. As we drove away I remarked to Stan, "I reckon that will be the car of somebody who is too poor to get it fixed by a 'real' mechanic."

"Certainly," said Stan. "Louis is still Louis."

EPILOGUE

I SUSPECT MANY PEOPLE experience what I do when they think back on the real characters who have graced their own lives; one recalls a name, the name bids up a face, and the remembered face lights up a present smile or prompts a chuckle. The faces of those it has been our privilege to know and learn from continue to shape us; the meaning in their persons has become part of our own sense of life's discernable meaning and hidden purposes both.

I find I can agree in part with Tennyson's "Ulysses," when Ulysses says "I am a part of all that I have met, / yet all experience is an arch wherethrough / gleams that untraveled world whose margins fade / forever and forever when I move." I say "in part" because I don't share Ulysses' unquenched wanderlust, just his acknowledgement that meaning in his own life is a composite of the innumerable gifts of wit and wisdom, burdens shared, tears and laughter alike, with others. We are never just ourselves, alone.

This little collection of tributes is woefully incomplete. There are so many others, many of whose admonitory or bracing impact on my sense of self and the world are far greater than those I have remembered here. A few of these were even "real characters" for whom a signature narrative might recall their uniqueness, their special gift.

Those closest to me may wonder, or even be disappointed, I suppose, that some of the more absurd episodes and adventures of my own mischief are here omitted. The reason is not so much my embarrassment as my desire to turn attention toward others more deserving and perhaps less well understood. Those who wish to seek written confirmation that I am neither saint nor sage can find a few confessions that have entered into my scholarly writing. I have put them there as necessary disclaimers; I am not the authority you seek, I have wanted to say, even as I have been doing my dead-level best to get some truth of history or poetry as close to right as my limited scope and tact would let me.

Every real character in this itinerary has been in some abiding sense my teacher. Among so many others are beloved family members, friends, and neighbors who have graced my way with wise sayings, aphorisms or proverbs, which have stuck, and many there be among my students and colleagues as well as kith and kin who have heard me repeat them, as often as not without attribution. Such is the truth in Ulysses' confession, and mine as well. We do not invent the language we speak; it, and its age-old speakers, speak through us still. I just hope that some good of their meaning comes through despite my inevitable hit and miss.

Made in the USA
Coppell, TX
06 July 2023

18834271R00080